American Red Cross Basic Water Safety and Emergency Water Safety Instructor's Manual

ISBN: 0-86536-148-7

Acknowledgments

The Lifesaving Revision Advisory Committee of the American Red Cross provided the primary advice and guidance for the design and content of this *Basic Water Safety and Emergency Water Safety Instructor's Manual.* The members of the committee included:

Reverend Rodney P. Bourg, St. Bernard Parish Chapter, Chalmette, Louisiana.

Paul M. Cerio, Supervisor of Aquatics, University of Nebraska, Omaha, Nebraska.

Darwin DeLappa, Director, Water Safety, NYS Parks, Recreation, and Historic Preservation, Albany, New York.

Michael C. Giles, Aquatics Director, University of Southern Mississippi, Hattiesburg, Mississippi.

Ralph Johnson, Ph.D., Associate Professor, Indiana University of Pennsylvania, Indiana, Pennsylvania.

John M. Malatak, Officer, Health and Safety, American Red Cross, national headquarters, Washington, D.C.

Jane W. McCharen, Metro Public Schools, Nashville, Tennessee.

Mike Miller, Director of Aquatics, University of Missouri, Kansas City, Missouri.

Kathryn Scott, Department of Physical Education, University of California at Berkeley, Berkeley, California.

Michael T. Shellito, Department of Parks and Recreation, City of Roseville, Roseville, California.

Marilyn Strom, Aquatics Director, University of Massachusetts-Boston, Boston, Massachusetts.

Royce Van Evera, Director of Community Services, American Red Cross, Albany Area Chapter, Albany, New York.

Lelia Vaughan, Recreation and Parks Consultant, Jonesville, Texas.

Members of the development team at the American Red Cross national headquarters included: Frank Carroll, Lawrence Newell, Ed.D., Heddy F. Reid, and Victoria A. Scott, M.P.A.

Contents

1 About Basic Water Safety and Emergency Water Safety

Introduction

The American Red Cross has been a leader in water safety since 1914. The primary purpose of the water safety program has been to help make people safe while they are in, on, and around the water. This instructor's manual is designed to be used by American Red Cross Water Safety Instructors and Lifeguard Training Instructors to teach two courses: Basic Water Safety and Emergency Water Safety. Both courses are aimed at helping people to be more safety conscious and better able to help themselves and others in the event of a water emergency. Although these courses have much in common, they are intended for different audiences.

Taking the Basic Water Safety course or the Emergency Water Safety course, or both, does not qualify a participant to be a lifeguard. Contact your local Red Cross for information on lifeguarding.

Purpose of the Basic Water Safety Course

The purpose of the Basic Water Safety course is to provide individuals, groups, and families with general water safety information, in order to create an awareness of causes and prevention of water accidents, to develop a desire to be safe, and to encourage healthy and safe water recreation.

Basic Water Safety focuses on personal and community water safety and may be taken by anyone of any age, regardless of swimming ability. People taking this course will receive a certificate of participation. Basic Water Safety is ideal, therefore, for families, scout troops, and other community groups or individuals interested in general water safety.

Purpose of the Emergency Water Safety Course

The purpose of the Emergency Water Safety course is to help participants to become fully familiar with potential hazards of water activities, to prevent accidents, and to respond effectively if an emergency does occur.

Emergency Water Safety, in contrast to Basic Water Safety, is intended only for people who already know how to swim well enough to pass a skills screening test. Emergency Water Safety is designed especially for individuals in the areas of recreation, education, public safety, and industry who want to know how to respond in an aquatic emergency. These include—

- People who participate in water recreation.
- People who enjoy hunting and fishing.
- Clubs and organizations interested in water activities.
- Police, firefighters, and emergency personnel who may work around water.
- Scout leaders.
- Industrial workers at water sites.
- Youth groups.
- Young people who wish to build a foundation for future courses in lifeguarding and aquatics.
- Owners of private ponds and swimming pools.

The Instructor's Manual

This instructor's manual is divided into three chapters and seven appendixes.
- Chapter 1 describes the Basic Water Safety course and the Emergency Water Safety course and provides information, guidelines, and suggestions for running both courses.
- Chapter 2 provides detailed information about the Basic Water Safety course. It includes three course outlines and three lesson plans that include classroom activities and water activities.
- Chapter 3 provides detailed information about the Emergency Water Safety course. It includes three course outlines and three lesson plans that include classroom activities and water activities.
- The appendixes include the following:
  — Appendix A, Water Skills Reference Guide for Instructors, is a quick poolside reference listing steps of all skills taught in the water.

— Appendix B, Skills Checklists, are checkoff sheets to keep a record of each student's progress.
— Appendix C, Equipment and Supplies List, is a comprehensive list of all the materials needed to teach each course.
— Appendix D, Additional Resources, includes a bibliography and list of externally produced audiovisuals that may be useful in preparing to teach these courses.
— Appendix E, Participant Course Evaluation, can be duplicated to use each time the instructor teaches the course.
— Appendix F, Instructor Course Evaluation, 2 copies per course. This form should be completed after the first and fourth times the instructor teaches the course.
— Appendix G, Emergency Water Safety Written Test Materials. Includes a 25-question written test and answer sheet for duplication, and an answer key.

Your Responsibilities as an Instructor

As an instructor of the Basic Water Safety and Emergency Water Safety courses, your responsibilities include the following:
- Being familiar with the course materials and knowing how to use them to teach effectively.
- Representing the American Red Cross in a positive manner.
- Explaining the importance of water safety education.
- Ensuring the safety of participants at all times.
- Encouraging participant success and enthusiasm.
- Managing the course and related administrative functions.
- Ensuring that the course environment, facilities, materials, and equipment are organized to enhance individual and group performance and to minimize distractions to the learning process.
- Evaluating participants' progress and correcting problems.
- Providing constructive feedback.
- Promoting other Red Cross courses and volunteer opportunities to course participants.

Setting Up and Running the Basic Water Safety and Emergency Water Safety Courses

Facilities
Each course includes classroom activities requiring dry land space with a writing surface for each person, and water activities requiring a swimming facility such as a pool or lake.

Adapting Lesson Plans for Scheduling of Facilities
Because it is not always possible to control the availability of facilities, the teaching outline is flexible. It may be necessary to rearrange the sequence of sessions or to devote an entire session to classroom activities and another to water activities.

Number of Participants
It is recommended that for every 10 participants in the class there be one instructor. If the class has more than 10 participants, there should be a co-instructor. Close supervision is required to ensure effective practice and the safety of participants. Furthermore, you can run a class more efficiently if you keep the class size reasonably small, and you are less likely to exceed the allotted time periods for various activities.

Equipment and Supplies
At the beginning of each session is a list of required equipment and supplies. A master list for all equipment for all basic and all emergency water safety sessions appears in Appendix C. Make sure all the equipment is ready and in working order before you teach the course.

Classroom Activities

Session Reviews
Each session (except the first) begins with a review of the previous session's content. Sample review questions are provided. Reviewing material provides an opportunity to—
- Reinforce important points in the lesson.
- Check on participants' understanding of the content.
- Enhance learning through repetition.
- Answer participants' questions about the material.
- Establish the link between the material previously taught and the current material.

Discussions

Discussions are frequently used to present material. Discussion, however, is not lecture or monologue. Discussions can include a variety of methods and materials such as—
- Questions and answers.
- Chalkboards or flip charts.
- Diagrams, charts, pictures, photographs, or water safety equipment.
- Anecdotes, case histories, examples, verbal illustrations, and newspaper clippings.

Audiovisuals

Various videos and films are suggested teaching aides for these courses. These are optional and, except for *Spinal Injury Management,* which is *strongly recommended,* are not included in the times suggested for each session. Appendix C, Equipment and Supplies, includes both the recommended and optional films and videos for the courses. Appendix D includes a list of externally-produced audiovisuals that may enhance the course.

Use of Case Histories

Descriptions of water safety incidents are provided at the beginning of some chapters in the *Basic Water Safety* text. Use these case histories as appropriate for motivation and illustration in any of the sessions, adding or substituting local stories as time permits.

Transition From Class to Water

Fifteen-minute breaks have been scheduled to give participants time to change into swimsuits and go to the swimming area. Before participants leave the classroom, wrap up class activities as follows:
- Summarize key points covered.
- Give the reading assignment for the next session.
- Briefly preview the skills to be practiced in the water.

Water Activities

Safety is an extremely important aspect of practice sessions. Every effort must be made to prevent accidents.
- A lifeguard (or safety lookout) should be on duty during the class.

- Basic Water Safety participants wearing PFDs for water activities must wear them at all times.
- Basic Water Safety participants who elect not to enter the water must not be allowed to play at the water's edge during practice sessions.
- Safety rules on running, ducking, dunking, or horseplay must be explained and enforced.
- All participants must be accounted for at the beginning and end of the session, and periodically throughout the session.
- The instructor must remain in the instructional area until all participants have been accounted for and have left.

All water activities include explanation and demonstration of the skill, followed by participant practice. Refer to *American Red Cross Swimming and Aquatics Safety* (Stock No. 321133) for class organization patterns for effective water practices and demonstrations.

For your quick reference, the steps of each water activity taught in Basic Water Safety and Emergency Water Safety are listed in Appendix B, Water Skills Reference Guide for Instructors, rather than in each session's lesson plan. You can photocopy the appendix and easily refer to it as you teach the water sessions.

Explanation and Demonstration

Demonstrate each water skill slowly and correctly, with an accompanying explanation, before participants attempt the skill. To ensure national standardization, instructors must demonstrate and teach the skills exactly as they appear in the audiovisuals, texts, and instructor's manual. If you use the audiovisuals, you do not need to repeat the skill demonstrations.

Practice

Design practice sessions so that each participant has maximum opportunity and ample space for practice. Make sure participants receive feedback on their efforts and offer suggestions for improvement, when necessary.

Organize water activities in such a way that participants do not have to enter and leave the water more often than necessary. Becoming chilled can be distracting and can interfere with the learning process.

Course Evaluations

Participants' evaluations of the course help to assess the teaching of the course, and suggest ways to improve future classes and courses. Evaluation is a continuing process throughout the course, and takes place naturally through spontaneous feedback from the participants. Their responses to instruction (whether they seem interested, bored, or confused, and whether they appear to understand what is taught) will give you some idea of your effectiveness as an instructor. In addition, written or oral evaluations at the end of the course can provide valuable information.

Written Evaluations

In the final session, ask participants to complete the Participant Course Evaluation Form (Appendix E). This is for feedback to the instructor and local Red Cross unit. The form can be photocopied for each participant and need not be signed, so comments can be anonymous.

Oral Evaluations

In some situations, for example, when members of the class are quite young, it may be appropriate to ask for oral feedback. Ask participants what they thought of the course, using the same questions that are on the written evaluation forms.

Instructor Course Evaluation

The Instructor Course Evaluation (Appendix F) asks your opinions about the course materials. You should fill it out the first and fourth times that you teach either course. Return the evaluation directly to:
    American Red Cross
    National Headquarters
    Health and Safety
    17th and D Streets, N.W.
    Washington, DC 20006
The information will help evaluate how well the course materials work for both new and experienced instructors.

2 *Basic Water Safety*

Course Length

Basic Water Safety has been designed to be taught in a minimum of nine hours. The course content is presented in three 3-hour sessions. Each session includes a classroom discussion followed by a 15-minute break. The water skills are demonstrated and explained by the instructor or video and then practiced by participants. If no boat (small craft) is available for use in Session 3, course length may be shortened by as much as 40 minutes.

Course Materials

In the beginning of each session is a list of the materials you will need for that specific class. Appendix C provides you with a complete list of all the equipment and supplies you will need to teach the course.

Participants

Both swimmers and nonswimmers may take Basic Water Safety. Participants must attend all sessions; however, their level of participation in water activities may vary. There are three levels of participation: (1) observers, nonswimmers who do not enter the water but can take part in many land activities, (2) PFD-wearers, participants who are comfortable in the water wearing a PFD, and (3) swimmers, participants who pass a skills screening test and can take part in water activities without a PFD. Participants should practice in shallow water only.

Skills Screening for Water Activities

During Session 1, ask participants whether they wish to take part in water activities. Those who wish to enter the water without a PFD must demonstrate the following skills:
1. Enter shallow water; swim into deep water next to edge of pool, dock, or lifeline for 10 yards; float or tread water for one minute; return to shallow water on the back.

2. Jump into deep water; level off; swim 10 yards to safety.

Participants who do not wish to enter the water may observe water activities from the water's edge and are encouraged and expected to practice water activities on land when appropriate. Listening to the instructor and observing the practice sessions increases an awareness and understanding of water safety.

Evaluating the Participants

There are no tests, neither skills tests nor written tests, at the end of the Basic Water Safety course. However, the instructor may use the Basic Water Safety Skills Checklist in Appendix B to check off the water activities skills completed.

Certificates

All people completing the course, both observers and in-water participants, may receive a course participation certificate (Cert. 3411).

Course Objectives

The objectives of both Basic Water Safety and Emergency Water Safety courses fall into three broad areas: (A) prevention, (B) self-help, and (C) helping others. Basic Water Safety skills are the foundation for the Emergency Water Safety course.

Note: Participants who do not enter the water will describe rather than demonstrate the skills performed in the water.

Objectives: Prevention
The following objectives focus on preventing hazardous situations in and near the water. At the end of the Basic Water Safety course, participants will be able to—
1. Identify major causes of water accidents.
2. Describe measures for preventing water accidents.
3. Identify major causes of water-related spinal injuries.
4. Identify the problems and preventive measures associated with exposure to cold water.
5. Discuss preventing ice accidents.

6. Describe self-rescue procedures for falling into cold water or through the ice.
7. Demonstrate proper way to put on a personal flotation device (PFD).
8. Board and debark a boat or small craft safely.*
9. Change positions in a boat or small craft safely.*

* These skills may be explained but not actually practiced, depending on the availability of equipment and on the participants' swimming ability.

Objectives: Self-Help

The following objectives focus on using self-help and survival techniques in the event of a water emergency. At the end of the Basic Water Safety course, participants will be able to—
1. Develop an emergency plan for a given situation.
2. Swim fully clothed.
3. Use clothes for flotation.
4. Demonstrate breath control and bobbing.
5. Perform survival floating.
6. Tread water.
7. Use the H.E.L.P. position.
8. Use the Huddle position.
9. Use an overturned boat or small craft for flotation.*
10. Reenter and hand-paddle a swamped boat or small craft.*

* These skills may be explained but not actually practiced, depending on the availability of equipment and on the participants' swimming ability.

Objectives: Helping Others

The following objectives focus on learning to use basic (non-swimming) methods of helping others in a water emergency. At the end of the Basic Water Safety course, participants will be able to—
1. Recognize and identify signs of a person in trouble in the water.
2. Demonstrate safe assists: reaching, throwing, and wading.
3. Analyze an emergency situation, select a safe and effective method of assisting, and call EMS.
4. Identify signs and symptoms of a spinal injury.
5. Demonstrate the hip and shoulder support technique for a victim of a suspected spinal injury.
6. Position a victim for rescue breathing and maintain an open airway on land and in shallow water.
7. Identify safe methods for assisting a person in a boating accident.

Basic Water Safety Course Outline

Session 1

Activity	Approximate Time	Method
Introductions and Discussion of Objectives	20 minutes	L/D
Prevention	15 minutes	L/D
Emergency Action Plans	10 minutes	L/D
Choosing a Safe Place to Swim	10 minutes	L/D
Hazards	15 minutes	L/D
Safety Tips for Other Water Activities	5 minutes	L/D
Self-Help in a Water Emergency	10 minutes	L/D
Optional Audiovisual: *Survival Swimming*	(8 minutes)	AV
Assignment and Break	15 minutes	
Water Activities Practice: Participant Safety and Skills Screening	30 minutes	Demo/P
PFDs	15 minutes	Demo/P
Sudden Immersion Skills	35 minutes	Demo/P

Session 1, Total Time   3 hours
(add 8 minutes for optional video)

AV = Audiovisual   D = Discussion
L = Lecture   P = Practice
Demo = Demonstration

Basic Water Safety Course Outline

Session 2

Activity	Approximate Time	Method
Review of Session 1 and Discussion of Objectives	15 minutes	L/D
Emergency Response: Helping Others	15 minutes	L/D
Optional Audiovisual: *Nonswimming Rescues*	(8 minutes)	AV
Spinal Injury Management Audiovisual: *Spinal Injury Management*	50 minutes including video	L/D/AV
Assignment and Break	15 minutes	
Water Activities Practice: Spinal Injury	20 minutes	Demo/P
Water Assists	45 minutes	Demo/P
Swimming Clothed and Inflating Clothes for Flotation	20 minutes	Demo/P

Session 2, Total Time   3 hours
(includes 25-minute video)
(add 8 minutes for optional video)

AV = Audiovisual　　　　　D = Discussion
L = Lecture　　　　　　　　P = Practice
Demo = Demonstration

Basic Water Safety Course Outline
Session 3

Activity	Approximate Time	Method
Review of Session 2 and Discussion of Objectives	15 minutes	L/D
Exposure to Cold Water	20 minutes	L/D
Ice Safety	10 minutes	L/D
Boating Safety	15 minutes	L/D
Optional Audiovisual: *Boating Safety and Rescues*	(11 minutes)	AV
Final Review	15 minutes	L/D
Break	15 minutes	
Water Activities Practice: H.E.L.P. Position/Huddle Position	15 minutes	Demo/P
Introduction to Rescue Breathing	25 minutes	Demo/P
Boating Safety	40 minutes	Demo/P
Course Review and Wrap-Up	10 minutes	L/D

Session 3, Total Time   3 hours
(add 11 minutes for optional video)

AV = Audiovisual
L = Lecture
Demo = Demonstration

D = Discussion
P = Practice

14

Basic Water Safety—Session 1
Lesson Plan

Suggested Time

3 hours

Topics

Introductions; prevention; emergency action plans; water hazards; safety tips; skills screening; PFDs; entries; self-help techniques; cramps.

Equipment

- Enrollment and registration materials
- Chalkboard and chalk or flip chart and markers
- *Basic Water Safety* textbook for each participant
- Wearable PFDs in good condition, 1 per participant
- 5 types of PFDs for display
- Appendix A, Water Skills Reference Guide for Instructors
- Audiovisual: *Survival Swimming* (8 minutes) (optional)
- Audiovisual projection equipment
- Appendix B: Basic Water Safety Skills Checklist

Facilities

Classroom, deck, or land for group discussions; pool, lake, or other swimming facility for water activities.

Objectives

At the end of Session 1, participants will be able to describe how to prevent hazardous situations in and near water, and will be able to describe or demonstrate self-help and survival techniques for water emergencies. Participants will be able to—
1. Identify major causes of water accidents.
2. Identify measures for preventing water accidents.

3. Develop an emergency plan for a given aquatic situation.
4. Identify safe responses to a sudden immersion.
5. Demonstrate the proper way to put on a personal flotation device (PFD).
6. Perform survival floating.
7. Tread water.

Note: Participants who do not enter the water will describe rather than demonstrate the water skills.

Introductions and Discussion of Objectives

**Suggested
Time**   20 minutes

Activity   Welcome participants and introduce all
teaching staff. Briefly point out the role and
history of the Red Cross in water safety
education.

Ask participants to explain their reasons for
taking the course and their expectations.
Explain whether or not this course will meet
participants' expectations.

Review with participants the course
purposes:
- To provide individuals and families with
  general water safety information in order to
  create an awareness of water accident
  causes and prevention.
- To develop a desire to be safe.
- To contribute to safe and healthy water
  recreation.

Emphasize the importance of being
prepared in water safety. Explain that by
knowing how to respond to potential dangers
in, on, and around water, participants may
prevent tragedy.

Describe course format and length:
- Meeting time and breaks.
- Attendance. To receive a course
  participation certificate, participants must
  attend all sessions. They must either
  observe or participate in the water
  activities.
- Clothing for water activities. Inform
  students when they must have clothes to
  wear in the water.
- Facility rules and regulations, such as
  smoking and eating.

- Textbook requirements and homework assignments.
- Describe the three levels of participation:
  - Observers, those who do not wish to enter the water and want to observe and participate in all activities that take place on land.
  - PFD-wearers or novice swimmers, those who do not feel totally comfortable in the water yet wish to participate in the water activities while wearing a PFD. They must wear a U.S. Coast Guard–approved PFD for all water activities. These participants will practice in water up to chest deep.
  - Swimmers, those who feel comfortable in deep water without a PFD and who have passed the skills screening for water activities.

Remind participants that course emphasis is on aquatic emergency responses that can be safely performed by nonswimmers and novice swimmers.

Note: Explain to observers that they can change to the PFD-wearer level for the second or third session if they want.

Discuss the course objectives for Session 1.

Prevention

Suggested Time 15 minutes

Activity Refer participants to page 2 of the textbook.
Cite statistics about the severity and extent of the water safety problem.

- About 6,000 Americans drown every year.
- Only motor vehicle accidents and falls cause more accidental deaths than drowning.
- Well over half of the drowning victims were doing something other than swimming or playing in the water when they drowned.
- Diving into shallow water results in the greatest number of serious spinal cord injuries of all sports.
- Diving into shallow water can result in complete paralysis from the neck down.

Point out that many of these deaths and serious injuries could be prevented if people would take a few simple precautions *before* swimming, diving, or playing.

Major Causes of Water Accidents
- Alcohol and drug use
- Diving into unknown water or water that is too shallow
- Overestimating ability and stamina
- Sudden immersion
- Small-craft accidents
- Medical emergencies

Ask participants what they think are the causes of most water accidents. List all the responses on the left side of a chalkboard or flip chart (leave room to add information on the right side of the list), finishing the list yourself, if necessary. Then discuss how and why each item listed presents a danger.

Discuss how to prevent water accidents. Ask participants how each cause listed could be prevented and write their responses on the right side of the list.

Point out that when an emergency happens, there is little time to analyze all the alternatives and decide what to do. A person who has thought in advance about what to do in case of emergency—even if that person is a nonswimmer—has the greatest chance of averting tragedy. The best way to be prepared for an emergency is to have a plan.

Emergency Action Plans

**Suggested
Time**   10 minutes

Activity   Refer participants to pages 3–6 of the textbook.
Discuss the elements of an emergency plan.

- A system of signals
- Safety equipment
- Development of site procedures

Also discuss the Emergency Medical Services (EMS) system in your community and how to access the system. (See the appendix on EMS in *Basic Water Safety,* pages 79–82.) Explain how to make make an emergency phone call and tell participants what information the dispatcher will need. It is important to post emergency information, such as telephone numbers and directions to the facility, near the phone because in a crisis it can be difficult to remember important details. Refer participants to the sample tear-out form, "Emergency Telephone Numbers," in the *Basic Water Safety* textbook appendix, page 83.

Explain the emergency plan for this facility. Explain the differences between the emergency plans for an indoor facility and for areas such as a beach or lakefront.

Give a local example of a nonlifeguarded area such as a pond, private pool, quarry, or lake. Ask participants to analyze what type of emergencies could happen and to develop an appropriate emergency plan for such an area.

Choosing a Safe Place to Swim

Suggested Time   10 minutes

Activity   Refer participants to page 6 and pages 20–22 of the textbook.

   Discuss characteristics of a safe place to swim and explain why each characteristic is important. Use the following scenarios and write participants' responses on the chalkboard or flip chart.

- You arrive at an unfamiliar pool (public or private). What are the safety conditions and characteristics to look for before you swim?

  Characteristics of a Safe Pool
  — Lifeguards
  — Clean water
  — Clean and well-maintained deck areas
  — Nonslip surfaces
  — Free of electrical equipment or power lines
  — Emergency communications to get help
  — Safety equipment
  — Water-depth markings
  — Buoyed lines separating shallow and deep water
  — Supervision for children and nonswimmers

- You are going swimming at a beach, lake, river, or ocean. What safety characteristics should you look for there?

  Characteristics of a Safe Beach
  — Lifeguards
  — Clean water
  — Clean and well-maintained beach
  — Sturdy docks, piers, and rafts with nonslip surfaces
  — Water-depth markings
  — Firm, gently sloping bottom

- — Free of electrical equipment or power lines
- — Emergency communication equipment
- — Safety equipment
- — Supervision for children and nonswimmers

Hazards

**Suggested
Time**   15 minutes

Activity   Refer participants to pages 8–19 of the
textbook.

Discuss potential hazards at waterfront
facilities (beaches, lakes, rivers). Note that
hazards differ around the country. Tell
participants to always check out a new area
before swimming. Emphasize hazards
common to your area and briefly summarize
other hazards.

Discuss each of the following hazards:
waves, currents, dams, aquatic plants and
animals, bottom hazards, bad weather, signs of
danger (flags, audible signals, absence of other
swimmers).

Explain what they are, how and why they
are dangerous, and what to do if you
encounter them.

Describe and diagram appropriate hazards.
(Don't label diagrams, so you can use them
later to check participants' knowledge.) Show
pictures or samples of various hazards.
Consult with fish, wildlife, or water recreation
agencies for supporting information and
materials.

Discuss the causes, prevention, and
treatment of each of the following hazards:
- Panic
- Cramps
- Exhaustion
- Hyperventilation
- Sunburn, heat stroke, heat exhaustion
- Hypothermia (you will discuss this in detail
  later)
- Inappropriate personal hygiene (clothing,
  hair) for swimming

Safety Tips for Other Water Activities

Suggested Time   5 minutes

Activity   Refer participants to pages 23–29 of the textbook.

     Review the safety tips for swimming, diving, and other recreational activities, as appropriate for the group. Focus only on those that pertain to the interests of the participants in your class (for example, infant and preschool swimming would be of greater interest to parents of toddlers than to teens or sports enthusiasts).

Self-Help in a Water Emergency

**Suggested
Time**   10 minutes

Activity   Refer participants to pages 36–37 of the
                  textbook.

                  Define sudden immersion and discuss
                  situations that might lead to suddenly finding
                  yourself in the water.

                  Explain that being near water is potentially
                  dangerous whether you plan to swim or not.
                  Explain that it is especially dangerous when
                  people don't plan to swim because they tend
                  to be less prepared.

                  Remind participants that—
                  • Accidental falls into water cause many of
                    the 6,000 drownings in the United States
                    each year.
                  • People are usually unprepared for such
                    falls, and they often panic if they are not
                    good swimmers.
                  • Wearing a PFD around water is the most
                    effective way to prevent drowning.
                  • Even if people fall into the water without a
                    PFD and are not strong swimmers, they
                    have a good chance to save themselves by
                    staying calm and using the survival
                    techniques taught in this session.

                  Cite one or more examples of immersion
                  situations in which safety precautions were not
                  followed, using local examples where possible.

Optional Audiovisual: "Survival Swimming"

Suggested Time   8 minutes

Activity   Show *Survival Swimming*.

Discuss safe responses to sudden immersion, including when to wait for help, when to try to reach safety, and what self-help techniques to use.

Assignment

Activity   Ask participants to read Chapters 1 and 2 in
the textbook for the next session, and tell
participants to bring clothes to wear in the
water, including a long-sleeved, button-down
shirt or blouse.

Break

**Suggested
Time**   15 minutes

Activity   Have participants change into swimsuits.

Water Activities Practice

Note: See Appendix A, Water Skills Reference
Guide for Instructors, for the steps of each
water skill to be taught and practiced in this
session. Use Appendix B, Basic Water Safety
Skills Checklist, to keep a record of
participants' progress.

Activity   Have participants prepare to go into the water.
Check to ensure that participants who are
required to wear PFDs for water activities have
put them on and fastened them correctly.

Participant Safety and Skills Screening

Suggested Time   30 minutes

Activity   Determine how participants wish to participate in the water sessions. There may be three levels:
- Participants who do not wish to participate in water sessions (observers)
- Participants who wish to participate while wearing a PFD (PFD-wearers)
- Participants who wish to participate fully in water activities without a PFD (swimmers)

Before any participants enter the water, discuss the pool or facility rules. Point out where the shallow and deep areas are.

Have participants enter shallow water, not deep water, until you feel comfortable with their abilities.

Conduct a skills screening. Participants who wish to take part in the water activities without wearing PFDs must perform the following skills:
1. Enter shallow water; swim 10 yards next to the dock or pool wall into deep water; float or tread water for one minute; return to shallow water on back.
2. Jump into deep water; level off; swim 10 yards to safety.

Participants who cannot perform these skills must wear PFDs for all water sessions. PFD-wearers should stay in water that is chest-deep or shallower.

Participants who do not want to enter the water may observe, join the discussions, take part in land activities, and practice water activities on the land. If they are going to be near the water's edge, they must wear a PFD.

- Prior to all practice sessions in the water, instructors must always make sure that participants requiring PFDs have put them on and fastened them properly. Remind participants wearing PFDs that they must not go into water deeper than chest level.

PFDs

**Suggested
Time**   15 minutes

Activity   Display 5 types of PFDs, if available, and
                explain their differences and specific uses.
                    Provide wearable PFDs to all participants.
                    Demonstrate how to put on a PFD and
                have participants practice.
                    Check each vest for proper fit and
                fastening.
                    Demonstrate how to ease into the water
                wearing a PFD. Demonstrate swimming in
                both prone and supine positions wearing a
                PFD.
                    Have participants wear PFDs and practice
                entering the water and swimming in chest-
                deep water.

Sudden Immersion Skills

Suggested Time

35 minutes

Activities

Refer participants to pages 39–40 of textbook. Use Appendix A, Water Skills Reference Guide for Instructors, for the steps of each water skill to be taught and practiced in this session.

Breath Control and Bobbing

Demonstrate breath control and bobbing in shallow water. Have participants enter shallow water and practice breath control and bobbing along with you. As participants become comfortable with the skill, progress to deeper water. PFD-wearers can practice by holding onto the edge of pool or dock and pushing themselves under water.

Floating on Back

Demonstrate floating on the back then add winging motion. Have swimmers practice floating on the back and then add winging and kicking in deep water. PFD-wearers can perform the exercise in shallow water.

Survival Floating

Explain the basis, purpose, limitations, and advantages of survival floating.

- Basis: The body has a natural tendency to swing down into a semivertical position with the head at or just below surface.
- Purpose: To help conserve energy while waiting for rescue. Movements should be slow and easy.
- Limitations: For use in warm water, not cold. Facedown floating causes the body to cool very quickly.

Demonstrate survival (facedown) floating. Have swimmers practice survival floating in deep water. PFD-wearers can simulate the exercise in chest-deep water. Observers can demonstrate the procedures on land.

Treading Water
Explain the purposes of treading water, and demonstrate how to tread water. Have swimmers practice treading water in deep water. PFD-wearers should practice in chest-deep or shallower water.

Releasing a Cramp
Demonstrate on the deck or land and in deep water how to work out a leg cramp. Have participants practice the technique on land and in shallow water.

End of Basic Water Safety Session 1

Basic Water Safety—Session 2

Lesson Plan

Suggested Time 3 hours

Topics Emergency response; safe diving; sudden immersion; swimming with clothes; reaching, throwing, and wading assists; spinal injuries.

Equipment
- Chalkboard and chalk or flip chart and markers
- *Basic Water Safety* textbook, 1 per participant
- Shepherd's crook
- Heaving line
- Throw bag
- Improvised reaching assist equipment
- PFDs as required for water activities
- *Spinal Injury Management* video (optional but strongly recommended)
- Optional *Nonswimming Rescues* audiovisual (8 minutes)
- Audiovisual projection equipment
- Appendix A, Water Skills Reference Guide for Instructors
- Appendix B, Basic Water Safety Skills Checklist

Facilities Classroom, deck, or land for group discussions; pool, lake, or other swimming facility for water activities.

Objectives At the end of Session 2, participants will be able to recognize when a person needs help in the water, demonstrate how to make a safe assist, and know the signs and symptoms of a spinal injury. Participants will be able to—
1. Recognize and identify signs of a person in trouble in the water.

2. Demonstrate safe assists for use by people who are not trained lifeguards.
3. Analyze a water emergency situation, select a safe and effective method of assisting, and call EMS.
4. Identify signs and symptoms of a spinal injury.
5. Swim fully clothed.
6. Use clothes for flotation.
7. Demonstrate the hip and shoulder support technique for a victim of a suspected spinal injury.

Review of Session 1 and Discussion of Objectives

Suggested Time

15 minutes

Activity

Select some questions from those below to provide a review of Session 1 and a transition into Session 2.

Sample review questions:

- How do alcohol and drug use affect water safety?
- What are some of the ways people push their limits in and around water?
- How can you avoid diving-related accidents?
- Why do activities around water sometimes end in tragedy? How can such tragedies be avoided?
- If you were invited to go out in a boat, how could you make sure the outing was as safe as possible?
- What does education have to do with water safety?
- What precautions should you take before you and your friends go swimming in an unsupervised area?
- What should you do if you begin to feel panicky in the water?
- When you find yourself suddenly and unexpectedly in water, what influences whether you stay and wait for rescue or try to reach safety?
- How do you perform survival (facedown) floating?

Discuss the objectives for Session 2.

Emergency Response: Helping Others

**Suggested
Time**   15 minutes

Activity   Refer participants to pages 43, 44, and 54 of
the textbook.

Emphasize the importance of being alert to
signs that someone may be in trouble.

Discuss signs that indicate if a person is—
- A tired swimmer.
- A person in distress.
- An active drowning victim.
- A passive drowning victim.

Discuss what a person needs to do when
helping someone in trouble in the water.
- Use your emergency action plan: evaluate
  the situation and determine your course of
  action.
- Call or send someone for emergency help.
- Determine what equipment is available and
  how many people can help.
- Maintain a safe position while you assist
  the victim.
- Don't endanger yourself.

Display the following rescue devices, giving
the name and purpose of each. Tell
participants they will be practicing with them
in the next water session.
- Shepherd's crook or reaching pole
- Heaving line
- Throw bag
- Ring buoy
- Rescue tube
- Improvised equipment, such as jug on a
  line, beach towel, belt, or oar

Explain that talking to the tired swimmer in a calm and reassuring voice is very important in any assist. The rescuer should tell the tired swimmer that help is coming and give instructions on what to do. This type of encouragement can often enable tired swimmers to help themselves.

Point out that during the practice activities participants should talk to the tired swimmer they are assisting.

Optional Audiovisual: "Nonswimming Rescues"

Suggested Time   8 minutes

Activity   Show the audiovisual and discuss it.

Spinal Injury Management

Suggested Time   50 minutes (including a 25-minute video)

Audiovisual   *Spinal Injury Management* is optional but strongly recommended. Showing the video *Spinal Injury Management* is recommended because it demonstrates and clarifies the technical maneuvers described in the text.

Activity   Show *Spinal Injury Management* .

After the video, have participants refer to the illustrations on pages 30–34 of the textbook as you reinforce key points.

Briefly discuss the anatomy and function of the spine.

Describe situations that may indicate spinal injury including the following:
- Any fall from a height greater than the victim's height
- Any person found unconscious or submerged in shallow water for unknown reasons
- Any significant head trauma
- All diving accidents

Review the signs and symptoms of a possible spinal injury including the following:
- Pain at the site of a fracture
- Loss of movement in the extremities above or below a fracture site
- Loss of feeling or tingling in the extremities
- Disorientation
- Neck or back deformity
- Visible bruising over an area of the spinal column
- Impaired breathing
- Head injury
- Fluid or blood in ears

Explain and discuss the general procedures for handling a suspected spinal injury in the water.

Emphasize the following general rescue procedures:
- Activate facility's emergency plan.
- Approach victim carefully. Minimize water movement. Do not jump or dive into a position near victim.
- Reduce or prevent any movement of victim's spine. Victim's head, neck, and back must be immobilized as much as possible. Use the hip and shoulder support technique.
- Move victim to the surface of the water, if necessary.
- Keep victim's face out of the water to allow victim to breathe.
- Move victim to shallow water, if possible.
- Check for breathing and maintain an open airway.

Assignment

Activity   Ask participants to read Chapters 3 and 4 in
the textbook for the next session.

Break

**Suggested
Time**   15 minutes

Activity   Have participants change into swimsuits.

Water Activities Practice

Note: See Appendix A, Water Skills Reference
Guide for Instructors, for the steps of each
water skill to be taught and practiced in this
session. See Appendix B, Basic Water Safety
Skills Checklist, to keep a record of participants'
progress.

Activity   Have participants prepare to go into the water.
Check to ensure that participants who are
required to wear PFDs for water activities have
put them on and fastened them correctly.

Spinal Injury

Suggested Time   20 minutes

Activity   Demonstrate the **hip and shoulder support technique**.
- Use in calm, shallow water only for faceup victims of suspected spinal injury when no help is immediately available to assist in boarding (placing the victim on a backboard).
- Have participants practice the skill. Participants take turns acting as the victim and the rescuer.

Water Assists

Suggested Time
45 minutes

Activity
Refer participants to pages 45–55 of the textbook.

Review the guidelines for making water assists to help someone in trouble.

- Activate your emergency action plan: evaluate the situation and determine your course of action.
- Call or send someone for emergency help.
- Determine what equipment is available and how many people can help.
- Maintain a safe position while you assist the victim.
- Maintain your grasp at the water's edge and keep your balance.
- Don't swim out to an active victim.
- Talk reassuringly to a tired swimmer or a person in distress, giving simple and concise directions.

Describe and demonstrate **reaching assists**.

- Describe and demonstrate a **reaching assist from land** using a long object (for example, a pole or branch).
- Describe and demonstrate a **reaching assist from the water**, while firmly grasping a secure object (for example, a pool ladder, overflow trough, or piling).

Have participants practice making reaching assists both in and out of the water while you observe.

- Give encouraging comments and suggestions as appropriate.

- When participants have mastered the basic maneuvers, position the victims just beyond reach so that rescuers have to improvise (for example, using a towel to extend reach during an assist from the water).
- Have participants practice water skills in depths in which they are comfortable and competent. All students must be carefully supervised in the water.

Describe and demonstrate assists for **submerged victims**.
- Point out that if a drowning victim is lying on the bottom and can be seen, a long reaching device can be used to recover the person. For example, use a shepherd's crook to encircle the victim or a boat hook to snag victim's clothing.
- Instruct participants that if victim cannot be seen or reached under water, they will have to direct the lifeguard or rescuers to the victim's position.
- If possible, sink an object (for example, knotted, weighted beach towels) to the bottom and demonstrate use of the shepherd's crook to recover it.
- Have participants practice recovering the sunken object with the shepherd's crook.

Describe and demonstrate **throwing assists**.
- Have all participants practice throwing the various devices to victims. Participants who are observing should wear a PFD when practicing this skill.

Describe and demonstrate **wading assists**.
- Review the techniques for making wading assists in shallow water with a flotation device.
- Review how to make a wading assist with a free-floating support.
- Have participants practice making wading assists.

Swimming Clothed and Inflating Clothes for Flotation

Suggested Time   20 minutes

Activity   Refer participants to pages 37–39 of textbook.

Put on clothing over a bathing suit and enter the water. Demonstrate swimming with clothes and demonstrate how to inflate a shirt by blowing and by splashing.

Have students enter shallow water with clothing over bathing suits and practice the skills listed below under close supervision.

- Swimming (using any combination of strokes that enables them to progress in the water and keep their faces out of the water)
- Inflating shirts by blowing
- Inflating shirts by splashing

End of Basic Water Safety Session 2

Basic Water Safety—Session 3

Lesson Plan

Suggested Time   3 hours

Topics   Ice safety; boating safety; exposure to cold; introduction to rescue breathing; and cold water survival techniques.

Equipment
- Chalkboard and chalk or flip chart and markers
- *Basic Water Safety* textbook, 1 per participant
- Film or video, *Boating Safety and Rescues* (11 minutes) (optional)
- Film or video projection equipment
- Throw bag or heaving jug
- Extra line
- Sound-signaling device—whistle, horn, or bell
- Visual distress signaling devices—flares or flags for daytime, flares or electric lights for nighttime
- Anchor
- First aid kit
- Bailing device
- Copies of local, state, and federal boating regulations
- Wearable PFDs, 1 per participant
- *Rescue Breathing and Choking Supplement* for instructor reference
- One or more small craft, such as a rowboat or canoe (optional)
- Appendix A, Basic Water Safety Skills Checklist
- Appendix B, Water Skills Reference Guide for Instructors

Facilities   Classroom, deck, or land for group discussions; pool, lake, or other swimming facility for water activities.

Objectives   At the end of this session, participants will be able to discuss prevention associated with exposure to cold and ice accidents, discuss hypothermia, and discuss prevention and safe methods for assisting in a boating accident. Participants will be able to—

1. Identify the problems and preventive measures associated with exposure to cold water.
2. Discuss preventing ice accidents.
3. Describe self-rescue procedures for falling through the ice or into cold water.
4. Describe measures for preventing and treating hypothermia.
5. Describe safe methods for assisting a person in a boating accident.
6. Describe how to board and debark a small craft safely.
7. Describe how to change positions in a small craft.
8. Use the H.E.L.P. and Huddle positions.
9. Describe how to use an overturned boat for flotation.
10. Describe how to reenter and hand-paddle a swamped boat.
11. Position a victim for rescue breathing and maintain an open airway on land and in shallow water.

Note: The water practice for the boating safety section is optional, depending on the availability of small craft for practice. However, boating safety must be discussed, and can be simulated in land drills.

Review of Session 2 and Discussion of Objectives

Suggested Time

15 minutes

Activity

Select some questions from those below to provide a review of Session 2 and a transition into Session 3.

Sample review questions:
- What are signs that a person is in distress in the water?
- What should you do when you see that someone needs help?
- What devices can be used to help someone in trouble in the water?
- Why is it important to talk to a victim?
- How can you maintain your own safety when helping someone else?
- Where should you aim when throwing a rescue device?
- How would you use a support if you were wading out to assist someone?
- What should you remember when making reaching assists?
- What objects can be used for a reaching assist?
- Why is checking water depth before entering the water so important?
- What are signs and symptoms of a spinal injury?
- What general rescue procedures apply to all spinal injury rescue techniques?
- When do you use hip and shoulder support?
- What should you do if you accidently fall into water?
- Why should you keep your clothes on if you fall into cold water?

Discuss the objectives for Session 3.

Exposure to Cold Water

Suggested Time 20 minutes

Activity Refer participants to pages 58–63 of the textbook.

Point out why knowing what to do when you or someone else falls into cold or icy water is vital.

- There is very little time to act.
- The cold very quickly reduces the victim's ability to act.

Cite an example of an accident of falling into cold water or falling through ice.

Define **hypothermia** and **cold water.**

- Describe what happens when hypothermia occurs. Mention that a victim of hypothermia may become unconscious and may die of heart failure.
- Explain that the amount of time a person can survive hypothermia without help depends on clothing, age, size, and body type. People with more body fat may survive longer than do children or elderly people.
- Discuss actions that can help prevent hypothermia:
  — Choose a safe place for recreation.
  — Be alert when near water.
  — Be sure there is help nearby before you participate in water activities.
  — Have PFDs and rescue devices in boats and around water or ice.
  — Wear rain gear or warm clothing in cool weather.
  — Don't drink alcohol to warm yourself.
  — Carry matches in waterproof container.
  — Never go near the water without someone with you.

- Review cold water survival self-help techniques for falling into cold water with and without a PFD.
  — Swimming clothed
  — Inflating clothes
  — Floating without putting face or head in water
  — Treading water
- Point out that even after a person gets out of cold water, danger is not past; it's important to act immediately to avoid hypothermia. Discuss self-help techniques once you are out of the water.
- Discuss procedures for helping another person who has been in cold water. Include procedures for helping a conscious victim and an unconscious victim.
  — Treat victim for shock.
  — Treat victim gently.
  — Stay with victim.
  — Observe victim carefully and monitor breathing.

Ice Safety

Suggested Time

10 minutes

Activity

Discuss how to tell whether ice is safe or unsafe. Include characteristics of safe ice and conditions that weaken ice.

Discuss guidelines for preventing ice accidents or minimizing their severity.

Explain safe responses to cracking ice:
1. Lie down immediately.
2. Spread arms and legs out to distribute weight evenly.
3. Crawl or roll to safety.

Explain that a standing person puts full weight on one spot, but when the person lies down, a larger area of ice supports that weight.

Discuss what to do if you fall through ice. Explain that while a natural response is to climb out, the ice might be weak around the edges and break off. Describe the correct procedures.

Discuss safe and unsafe action to take when someone else falls through ice. Remind participants not to go on the ice themselves when making a rescue.

Ask participants to identify the assists they would use and why.

Boating Safety

Suggested Time   15 minutes

Activity   Refer participants to pages 48–49 of the textbook.

Point out that U.S. waterways are second only to highways as the scene of transportation deaths. Determine how many in the class have been in or around small craft (16 feet or less) and ask—

- Have you witnessed any dangerous situations?
- What happened and what were the outcomes?
- What might have caused the situation?
- How could the danger have been prevented?

Describe a boating accident. Discuss causes and prevention measures.

Discuss the importance of being prepared for safe boating.

Recommend that all boaters should learn how to swim.

- Stress Red Cross swimming instruction.
- Discuss how to find out about local programs and schedules.

Tell participants that all boaters should be able to handle small craft.

- Compare using a boat without instruction to driving a car without instruction.
- Note courses offered by local organizations (for example, the American Red Cross, U.S. Coast Guard Auxiliary, U.S. Power Squadron, U.S. Yacht Racing Union, American Canoe Association).

Stress that everyone should wear a Coast Guard–approved PFD while boating, regardless of swimming ability.

Discuss the dangers of drinking and using drugs while boating.
- Lessens your ability to handle a boat.
- Affects balance judgment.
- Inhibits the body's ability to stay warm.
- Reduces swimming abilities.

Review safe locations and conditions for boating:
- Away from swimming areas.
- Clear weather reports.
- Separate docking facilities for small boats.

Discuss and display, if possible, the minimum safety equipment for small craft. (See section *Equipping Your Boat* in Chapter 4 of the textbook.) If available, give participants local, state, or federal boating requirements or explain how participants can get copies.

Optional Audiovisual: "Boating Safety and Rescues"

Suggested Time   11 minutes

Activity   Show the audiovisual and discuss it.

Final Review

15 minutes

Note: This is the last review in the Basic Water Safety course. It is placed here so participants can review the material before they change into swimsuits and go to the water activities.

Activity

Use the following review questions, and any other review questions you wish, to recap the entire course.

- What safety precautions can help prevent or minimize effects of cold water exposure?
- What should you do if you fall into cold water?
- How can you help someone who has fallen into cold water?
- What should you do after helping someone out of cold water?
- How can you prevent ice accidents?
- What should you do if you fall through the ice?
- How can you help someone who has fallen through the ice?
- Why is it important to act very quickly in a cold water or ice emergency?
- How does using alcohol increase the risk of boating accidents?
- Who should wear PFDs when in a boat?
- Under what conditions is it safe to drive or ride in small craft?
- What are the basic navigation "rules" for boating?
- What does it mean to trim a boat, and why is it important?
- Under what conditions would you leave a capsized craft and swim to shore?
- Of the assists you have learned, which can you use from a small craft?

Break

**Suggested
Time**   15 minutes

Activity   Have participants change into swimsuits.

Water Activities Practice

Note: See Appendix A, Water Skills Reference
Guide for Instructors, for the steps of each
water skill to be taught and practiced in this
session. See Appendix B, Basic Water Safety
Skills Checklist, to keep a record of participants'
progress.

Activity   Have participants prepare to go into the water.
Check to ensure that participants who are
required to wear PFDs for water activities have
put them on and fastened them correctly.

H.E.L.P. Position and Huddle Position

Suggested Time

15 minutes

Activity

Refer participants to page 61 of the textbook.
Wearing a PFD, explain and demonstrate the **H.E.L.P.** (Heat Escape Lessening Posture) position.

- Have all participants wear a PFD and practice the H.E.L.P. position in warm, shallow water.

Wearing a PFD, explain and demonstrate the **Huddle Position**.

- Have participants wear a PFD and divide into groups to practice the Huddle position in warm, chest-deep water.

Introduction to Rescue Breathing

Suggested Time   25 minutes

Instructor reference: *American Red Cross Rescue Breathing and Choking Supplement,* pages 1–5, for hand positions and sequencing.

Activity   Explain that the act of opening the airway and maintaining an open airway frequently is sufficient to help the victim begin breathing on his or her own.

Explain that in this course, participants will learn opening the airway and positioning the victim for rescue breathing on land and in the water. They can learn more about how to perform rescue breathing in the Emergency Water Safety course. Complete steps for performing rescue breathing are taught in American Red Cross CPR and first aid courses.

Demonstrate the procedure for opening the airway following the steps outlined in the Supplement.

Introduce Rescue Breathing practice.
- Explain that one person will be a victim and one person will be a rescuer. After participants practice the skill once, they will change places.
- Remind participants that, when practicing with a partner, they *will not* make mouth-to-mouth contact or give actual rescue breaths.
- Lead participants through the practice with the following steps:
  1. Assign partners or tell participants to find partners and decide who will be the victim and who will be the rescuer.
  2. Tell the victims to lie on the floor on their stomachs. Their heads should all be pointed in the same direction, for example, toward the wall or toward the water.

3. Using the steps in the *Rescue Breathing and Choking Supplement*, pages 1–5, guide the rescuers through the following steps:
   — Check for unresponsiveness.
   — Position the victim.
   — Open the airway.
   — Check for breathlessness. During the check for breathlessness, tell the victims to breathe normally so the rescuers can see the chest rise and fall, and listen and feel for escaping air. Then ask the victims to hold their breath briefly so the rescuers can see the difference between a breathing and a nonbreathing (breathless) victim.
   — Tell someone to phone the EMS system for help.
4. Reverse the victim and the rescuer roles. Lead the new rescuers through the same steps.
5. Explain and demonstrate how to give rescue breathing in shallow water, even though participants will not practice this part of the skill.
6. Have participants practice opening the airway, checking for breathing, and positioning the victim for breathing in shallow water.
7. Have participants practice with and without using the edge of the pool as a solid support.

Boating Safety

**Suggested
Time**   40 minutes

Note: Use a small boat or canoe if available for these activities. However, if no small craft is available, the procedures can be explained and demonstrated using whatever props are handy. For example, a beach towel can serve as the boat bottom and a kickboard held on edge as the side of the boat. Simulate the activities in a land drill.

Activity   Point out and name the main parts of a boat, using a boat or canoe, or a picture or diagram.

Explain **trimming a boat**, balancing the weight from side to side and from front to back.

Discuss preparations and procedures for **boarding a boat**.

Explain and demonstrate procedures for **boarding and debarking**.

Explain and demonstrate how to **change positions** in a boat.

Have participants practice boarding, trimming, changing positions, and debarking while wearing PFDs.

Ask students what they would do if their boat capsized or swamped in a lake.

Explain and demonstrate how to reenter a swamped boat. Partially fill the craft with water and use an assistant to help demonstrate.

Have participants practice reentering and hand-paddling a swamped boat while wearing PFDs.

Discuss what to do from a boat to assist a victim in the water.

Review precautions to take when making an assist from a boat.

Have participants practice making a

throwing assist from a boat.

Refer participants to American Red Cross boating safety textbooks for additional suggestions on safe procedures for small craft.

Demonstrate how to reach and throw from a boat and help someone aboard. Caution participants that standing up in a small craft could easily tip the craft over. When possible, reach or throw from a sitting position.

Have participants practice—
- Reaching from a boat.
- Throwing a device on a line.
- Helping a victim aboard.

3 *Emergency Water Safety*

Course Prerequisites

To be eligible for the Emergency Water Safety course, the candidate must present an American Red Cross Intermediate Swimming certificate or successfully pass a screening test consisting of the following swimming skills:
- Swim continuously for 5 minutes while performing the crawl stroke and sidestroke for a minimum of 50 yards each.
- Jump into deep water, swim approximately four body lengths underwater, surface, and tread water for one minute.

The candidate must also demonstrate competency in Basic Water Safety skills, including the following sudden immersion skills and water assists:
- Reaching assist
- Throwing assist
- Wading assist
- Survival (facedown) floating

It is *strongly recommended* that participants complete the Basic Water Safety course before they take the Emergency Water Safety course.

Course Length

Emergency Water Safety has been designed to be taught in 9 hours or less. This time includes the showing of one video. The course is presented in three 3-hour sessions. The unit on masks, fins, and snorkels at the end of Session 3 is optional depending on the needs of the participants, and has not been included in the total course times.

Although Basic Water Safety is not a prerequisite for this course, the Basic Water Safety course is the foundation of the Emergency Water Safety course. If participants have not recently completed, or have never taken, a Basic Water Safety course, you may need to build more time into the Emergency Water Safety course to teach and review elementary rescue skills and water safety and prevention information.

Course Materials

At the beginning of each session is a list of required equipment and supplies for teaching that session. A master list of equipment and supplies for all Basic and all Emergency Water Safety sessions appears in Appendix C. Make sure all equipment is ready and in working order before you teach the course.

Adapting Lesson Plans for Participants' Needs and Interests

For classes made up of special interest groups, you may wish to adapt the content of the sessions by emphasizing portions that are of particular interest to the group and shortening less relevant parts. For example, for people who enjoy hunting and fishing, you might concentrate on water hazards, sudden immersion, exposure to ice and cold, and boating safety, and reduce the time spent on pool safety and diving. For parents, you might focus on backyard pool safety and safe conditions for swimming.

It is a good idea to spend some time in the first session learning about participants' interests so that you can tailor the course to their needs.

Testing and Certificates

To be eligible for a course completion certificate, participants must score at least 80 percent on the written test consisting of 25 questions and successfully perform the four combined skills in the water skills test.

When providing feedback on the exam, do not answer a particular test question, but instead make your answer general. Do **not** return the answer sheets to the participants. Participants who pass the final skills tests and the written test will receive a course completion certificate (Cert. 3413).

Grading Criteria

On the *Course Record* (Form 6418) enter a grade of pass, fail, or incomplete for each participant. "Pass" (P) should be entered for the participant who has passed the four skills in the skills test and scored at least 80 percent on the written test. "Fail" (F) should be entered as the final grade for a participant who has not passed **all** the required skills and the written test. "Incomplete" (I) should be entered as the final grade if the participant is unable to complete the course due to circumstances such as illness.

Course Objectives

The Emergency Water Safety course builds on the goals and shares the objectives of the Basic Water Safety course, and also has other objectives specific to the content and scope of the Emergency Water Safety course.

At the end of the course, participants will be able to—
1. Submerge and swim underwater.
2. Describe when rescue breathing is necessary.
3. Describe how to perform rescue breathing on an adult.
4. Position a victim for rescue breathing on an adult.
5. Perform a feetfirst surface dive in shallow and deep water.
6. Perform a pike surface dive and swim underwater.
7. Take part in a human chain to assist a victim in the water.
8. Enter deep water using a stride jump.
9. Jump into deep water.
10. Get in position to assist a victim.
11. Demonstrate towing a victim to safety using a rescue tube.
12. Demonstrate towing a passive victim to safety using the wrist tow.
13. Demonstrate towing a passive victim to safety using the armpit tow.
14. Describe the signs and symptoms of a spinal injury.
15. Describe the general rescue procedures for the victim of a suspected spinal injury.
16. Provide hip and shoulder support for the victim of a suspected spinal injury.
17. Stabilize the victim of a suspected spinal injury using the head splint technique.
18. Put a victim on a backboard, apply a cervical collar, strap the victim, and remove the board from the water.
19. Remove a victim from water using a shallow water assist.
20. Remove a victim from water using a drag assist.
21. Remove a victim from water by lifting.
22. Escape from a panicky victim's grasp on the head, arm, or wrist.
23. Demonstrate surface dives to recover a submerged victim.

Optional Objectives

At the end of Session 3 participants will be able to—
1. Identify characteristics of good masks and fins.
2. Identify safe practices for swimming with mask, fins, and snorkel.
3. Put on mask, fins, and snorkel properly.
4. Clear a mask.
5. Equalize pressure in mask and ears.
6. Clear a snorkel.
7. Enter water with mask, fins, and snorkel using a sit-in entry.
8. Enter water with mask, fins, and snorkel using a stride-jump entry.
9. Swim with mask, fins, and snorkel.
10. Identify criteria for selecting mask, fins, and snorkel.

Emergency Water Safety Course Outline

Session 1

Activity	Approximate Time	Method
Skills Screening	30 minutes	P
Introductions and Discussion of Objectives	20 minutes	L/D
Understanding Drowning	10 minutes	L/D
Water Assists	5 minutes	L/D
Assignment and Break	15 minutes	
Water Activities Practice: Human Chain	15 minutes	Demo/P
Water Entries	20 minutes	Demo/P
Positioning	15 minutes	Demo/P
Tows	50 minutes	Demo/P

Session 1, Total Time   3 hours

AV = Audiovisual

L = Lecture

Demo = Demonstration

D = Discussion

P = Practice

Emergency Water Safety Course Outline

Session 2

Activity	Approximate Time	Method
Review of Session 1 and Discussion of Objectives	10 minutes	L/D

Rescue Breathing
    Audiovisual: *What to Do When*
        Breathing Stops
	70 minutes
	including video
		L/D
		
		AV

Assignment and Break	15 minutes	

Water Activities Practice:
    Rescue Breathing in
    Shallow and Deep Water
	20 minutes	Demo/P

Recovery of Submerged Victim
    Surface Diving
    Swimming Underwater
    Recovery
	25 minutes	Demo/P

Escapes	20 minutes	Demo/P
Removal From Water	20 minutes	Demo/P

Session 2, Total Time   3 hours
(includes 10-minute video)

AV = Audiovisual   D = Discussion

L = Lecture   P = Practice

Demo = Demonstration

Emergency Water Safety Course Outline

Session 3

Activity	Approximate Time	Method
Review of Session 2 and Discussion of Objectives	5 minutes	L/D
Spinal Injury Audiovisual: *Spinal Injury Management*	35 minutes including video	L/AV
Break	15 minutes	
Water Activities Practice: Spinal Injury Management	60 minutes	Demo/P
Testing Skills Test Written Test	35 minutes 20 minutes	T Demo/T
Evaluation, Administration, and Wrap-Up	10 minutes	L/D

Session 3, Total Time   **3 hours**
(includes 25-minute video)

Optional Session

Activity	Approximate Time	Method
Optional Audiovisual: *Snorkeling Skills and Rescue Techniques*	(13 minutes)	AV
Mask, Fins, and Snorkel	15 minutes	L/D
Break	10 minutes	
Water Activities Practice: Mask and Snorkel Fins Water Entries With Equipment Swimming With Equipment	10 minutes 10 minutes 10 minutes 15 minutes	Demo/P Demo/P Demo/P Demo/P

Optional Session, Total Time   **1 hour, 10 minutes**
(add 13 minutes for audiovisual)

AV = Audiovisual
L = Lecture
Demo = Demonstration

D = Discussion
P = Practice
T = Test

Emergency Water Safety—Session 1

Lesson Plan

Suggested Time
3 hours

Topics
Skills screening; discussion of objectives; understanding drowning; water assists; entries; positioning; tows.

Equipment
- Enrollment and registration materials
- Chalkboard and chalk or flip chart and markers
- *Basic Water Safety* textbook, 1 per participant
- *Emergency Water Safety* textbook, 1 per participant
- Rescue tubes and ring buoys, 1 per every 3 to 4 participants

Facilities
Classroom, deck, or land for group discussions; pool, lake, or other swimming facility for water activities

Objectives
At the end of Session 1, participants will be able to describe the difference between an active and passive drowning victim, and be able to describe or demonstrate various techniques for assisting or rescuing a passive victim.

Participants will—
1. Enter deep water using a stride jump.
2. Enter deep water using a feetfirst jump.
3. Demonstrate a human chain with other participants.
4. Get in position to assist a victim.
5. Tow a victim to safety using a rescue tube.
6. Tow a victim to safety by the wrist.
7. Tow a victim to safety by the armpit.

Skills Screening

Suggested Time

30 minutes

Activity

If participants do not have an American Red Cross Intermediate Swimming certificate, you must test their ability to do the following:
1. Swim continuously for five minutes while performing the crawl stroke and sidestroke for a minimum of 50 yards each.
2. Jump into deep water, swim approximately four body lengths underwater, surface, and tread water for one minute.

In addition, participants must demonstrate their competency in the following Basic Water Safety skills:
1. Make a reaching assist from land by extending one hand.
2. Make a throwing assist using a ring buoy with a line.
3. Make a wading assist using a ring buoy or a rescue tube as a supporting device.
4. Demonstrate survival (facedown) floating for one minute.

Anybody who cannot pass the skills screening may not take part in the course. Suggest that these candidates enroll in an American Red Cross Intermediate Swimming course or appropriate-level course.

Introductions and Discussion of Objectives

Suggested Time　　20 minutes

Activity　　Welcome participants and introduce all teaching staff. Briefly point out the role and history of the Red Cross in water safety education.

Ask participants to explain briefly their reasons for taking the course and their expectations.

Explain the course purposes:
- To help participants become fully familiar with potential hazards of water activities
- To prevent water accidents
- To respond effectively in an emergency

Emphasize that although participants will learn how to assist passive victims and tired swimmers, *this course does not teach lifeguarding skills.*

Discuss the objectives for the session.

Understanding Drowning

Suggested Time

10 minutes

Activity

Refer participants to pages 5–6 of the textbook.
Review How to Help Others: Reach, Throw, and Wade in Chapter 2, *Basic Water Safety*, pages 43–55.
Explain asphyxiation.
Describe an active drowning victim:
- Struggles in the water
- Usually unable to call for help
- Usually struggles briefly and violently, breathes in water, and may slip underwater and become a passive drowning victim

Describe a passive drowning victim:
- May or may not have been an active victim
- Slips underwater or floats facedown on or near surface
- Often unnoticed by persons nearby

Point out that knowing how to assist a passive victim or a tired swimmer can make the difference between life and death. To perform a water assist, you must—
- Be a strong swimmer.
- Have skills acquired through training and practice.
- Have good judgment to decide when to try a water assist and when to get emergency assistance. Remind participants that in this course they will be learning assists for passive victims. They are not learning lifeguarding skills in this class.

Have participants evaluate the following situation:

You are a strong swimmer. You notice that someone who was just thrashing about in the water is now oddly still and floating facedown. No lifeguard is close by.

- Ask participants what factors would influence how they help the victim.
- Write their ideas on the chalkboard or flip chart.

Discuss the factors to consider in helping someone in an emergency situation:

- Condition of victim, active or passive
- Distance to victim
- Available equipment
- Available lifeguards and bystanders
- Water depth
- Weather and water conditions

Refer back to the situation described previously and add any other factors to the list on the chalkboard or flip chart.

Have participants evaluate the next situation:

You are a strong swimmer. You notice that someone about 20 feet from the dock is thrashing about and has a panicked expression. No lifeguards are nearby.

- Ask participants what factors influence how to help the person.
  - Emphasize that to assist an active victim, you need strong, well-practiced skills.
  - Remind participants to summon lifeguards or call EMS.
  - Rescuers must fix (sight) the position of the victim.

Water Assists

Suggested Time   5 minutes

Activity   Refer participants to pages 7–9 of the textbook.

Discuss using a water assist to help a passive victim and a tired swimmer.

Explain that it is important to always use a flotation device while making a rescue. A rescuer must evaluate the situation and know what conditions would make it dangerous to attempt an assist.

- Bad weather
- Poor water conditions
- Too great a distance to victim

Remind participants again that the best decision may be for someone to call a lifeguard or EMS while another person keeps watching the person in trouble to report where the victim was last seen.

Assignment

Activity   Give the reading assignment for next class: Chapter 1 in the *Emergency Water Safety* textbook, the *American Red Cross Rescue Breathing and Choking Supplement,* and a review of Chapters 1 and 2 in the *Basic Water Safety* textbook.

Review the skills to be taught in the water activities.

Break

Suggested Time   15 minutes

Activity   Have participants get ready to enter the water. (They will already be in their swimsuits from the skills screening.)

Water Activities Practice

Note: See Appendix A, Water Skills Reference Guide for Instructors, for the steps of each water skill to be taught and practiced in this session. See Appendix B, Emergency Water Safety Skills Checklist, to keep a record of participants' progress.

Human Chain

Suggested Time
15 minutes

Activity
Explain that the human chain can be used when enough people are available to help form a chain and when the water is not above chest level nor fast moving. Describe the steps as listed in Appendix A, Water Skills Reference Guide for Instructors.

Water Entries

20 minutes

Activity

Refer participants to pages 8–9 in the textbook. See Appendix A, Water Skills Reference Guide for Instructors, for the steps of each water skill to be taught and practiced in this session.
Explain and demonstrate three entries:

- **Ease into the water**
  This entry keeps water movement from jarring victim's body and must be used if neck or spinal injury is suspected.
  Use this entry when the water is shallow or the depth unknown.

- **Stride-jump entry**
  Use this entry in water at least 5 feet deep when rescuer is 3 feet or less above surface.

- **Feetfirst-jump entry**
  This entry is a good choice when water depth is known and rescuer is no more than 5 feet above the surface.

Have participants practice each of the three entries.

Positioning

**Suggested
Time**   15 minutes

Activity   Refer participants to page 9 of the textbook.
        Explain and demonstrate how to swim to a
victim and how to move into a position of
safety in order to help a passive victim.
        Have participants walk through positioning
on land first, then have participants position
themselves as victims in the water wearing
PFDs. Have other participants (as rescuers)
approach them from different directions and
practice moving into a safety position.
        Reverse victim and rescuer roles.

Tows

Suggested Time   50 minutes

Activity   Refer participants to pages 9–13 in the textbook.

Describe and demonstrate the following tows:

- **Wrist tow**
  Wrist tow is good for long distances, and lets rescuer keep control of victim.
- **Single armpit tow**
  Single armpit tow also allows rescuer to control victim.
- **Rescue tube tow**
  Rescue tube maintains distance between rescuer and victim, and there is no contact with victim.

Have participants practice doing all the tows with different partners.

Encourage participants to use the practice session to judge the effectiveness of the various tows with different sizes of victims.

If necessary, work with participants individually to determine pulls and kicks they can use effectively.

Note: The collar tow and changing positions may also be taught if time allows.

End of Emergency Water Safety Session 1

Emergency Water Safety—Session 2

Lesson Plan

**Suggested
Time**   3 hours

Topics   Rescue breathing in shallow and deep water;
                surface dives, swimming underwater; recovery
                of a submerged victim; escapes; removal of
                victim from the water.

Equipment   • *Basic Water Safety* textbook, 1 per
                  participant.
                • *Emergency Water Safety* textbook, 1 per
                  participant.
                • *American Red Cross Rescue Breathing and
                  Choking Supplement,* 1 per participant.
                • Strongly recommended video: *American
                  Red Cross: Adult CPR* or *American Red
                  Cross Community CPR* .
                • Video projection equipment.
                • Manikins, 1 per 2 to 3 participants, and
                  manikin decontamination solution.
                  (Manikin decontamination solution: one-
                  quarter cup liquid household chlorine
                  bleach per gallon of tap water. The
                  solution must be made fresh just prior to
                  each class and discarded after use.)
                • Clean gauze pads (4" x 4"), a baby bottle
                  brush, soap and water, basins or buckets,
                  nonsterile disposable gloves, and other
                  supplies recommended by the manikin
                  manufacturer for manikin decontamination.

Facilities Classroom, deck, or land for group discussions;
                pool, lake, or other swimming facility for water
                activities.

Objectives When they finish this session, participants will
                be able to position a victim for rescue

breathing in shallow and deep water; describe how to perform rescue breathing; perform surface dives and swim underwater; and remove a victim from the water.

Specifically, participants will be able to—

1. Describe when rescue breathing is necessary.
2. Describe how to perform rescue breathing on an adult.
3. Position a victim for rescue breathing in shallow and deep water.
4. Perform a feetfirst surface dive and swim underwater.
5. Perform a pike surface dive and swim underwater.
6. Escape from a panicky victim's grasp on the head, arm, or wrist.
7. Remove a victim from the water using a shallow water assist.
8. Remove a victim from the water using a drag assist.
9. Remove a victim from the water by using a lift.

Review of Session 1
and Discussion of Objectives

**Suggested
Time**   10 minutes

Activity   Select some questions from those below to
                provide a review of Session 1 and a transition
                into Session 2.
- What factors should you consider when
  evaluating a water emergency? Why is
  each factor important?
- What are the steps in a water assist?
- Under what conditions should you NOT try
  a water assist?
- What are the advantages of a stride-jump
  entry?
- In what situation would a feetfirst entry be
  a good choice?
- When should you enter the water by easing
  in?
- How would you position yourself to assist
  a passive victim?
- Why should towing a victim to safety be
  attempted only by a strong swimmer?

Discuss the objectives for Session 2.

Rescue Breathing

Suggested Time

70 minutes (includes a 10-minute video)

Audiovisual

What to Do When Breathing Stops is optional but strongly recommended because it demonstrates and clarifies rescue breathing.

Activity

Show *What to Do When Breathing Stops,* the rescue breathing segment of the *American Red Cross Adult CPR* or *Community CPR* video. Discuss the EMS system in your community and how to make an emergency phone call. (Refer participants to the appendix in the *Basic Water Safety* textbook.)

Demonstrate the proper way to decontaminate manikins after each use. The decontamination solution ingredients are listed in the Equipment and Supplies List in Appendix C. For complete manikin decontamination guidelines refer to Appendix A of the *American Red Cross CPR Instructor's Manual.*

During class, the decontamination solution must be applied with clean 4" x 4" gauze pads. To decontaminate the manikins after class, you will need, in addition to the decontamination solution and gauze pads, a baby bottle brush, soap and water, basins or buckets, nonsterile disposable gloves, and other supplies recommended by the manikin manufacturer.

Tell participants not to use the manikin if:
- They have any cuts or sores on their hands, head, lips, or mouth (for example, cold sores).
- They have ever had a positive test for hepatitis.
- They have any respiratory infections such as a cold or sore throat.

Note: Because it is possible that some instructors may not have taught rescue breathing, the following detailed directions are provided. Urge participants to enroll in an American Red Cross Adult CPR or Community CPR course if they want to learn CPR.

Activity   Introduce rescue breathing practice.

Explain that one person will be a victim, and one person will be a rescuer. After they practice the skill once, they will change places so that they each have a chance to be a rescuer.

Remind them that, when practicing with a partner, they *should not* make mouth-to-mouth contact and *should not* give breaths.

Practice on a partner

Lead participants through a practice as follows:

1. Move participants into a practice area on land.
2. Assign partners or tell them to find partners.
3. Tell the victims to lie on their stomachs. Their heads should all be pointed in the same direction, for example, toward the wall or toward the water.
4. Using the steps in the *Rescue Breathing and Choking Supplement* (pages 1–8), guide the rescuers through the following steps:
   - Check for unresponsiveness.
   - Position the victim.
   - Open the airway.
   - Check for breathlessness. During the check for breathlessness, tell the victims to breathe normally so the rescuers can see the chest rise and fall, and listen and feel for escaping air. Then tell the victims to hold their breath briefly so

the rescuers can see the difference between a breathing and a nonbreathing (breathless) victim.

- Simulate rescue breaths. Remind participants not to give actual rescue breaths to their partner. They should simulate breathing into the victim by turning their head away from the victim's face and blowing towards the chest using the correct timing.
- Check for pulse.
- Ask someone to phone the EMS system for help.

5. After you have completed this practice, have the participants reverse roles. Lead the new rescuers through the same steps.

Practice on a manikin
Lead participants through a practice as follows:
1. Take the manikins out of their cases. The manikins should be placed on their backs. Tell participants not to practice "positioning the victim" with a manikin. They should leave the manikins on their backs in order to keep the faces clean. Tell them to check for unresponsiveness and then open the airway.
2. Before participants start practicing on the manikins, demonstrate the correct way to clean the manikin's face each time a different person starts to practice on the manikin.
3. Lead participants through rescue breathing practice as described on pages 1–8 in the *Rescue Breathing Supplement*.

At the end of practice on a partner or a manikin
Check to make sure each participant knows how to do the rescue breathing skills.

Have participants answer the review
questions in the *Rescue Breathing Supplement*
on page 9 (answers on page 10).

Assignment

Activity   Ask participants to read Chapter 3 in the text
and review Diving Safety in Chapter 1 of the
Basic Water Safety text.

Break

**Suggested
Time**   15 minutes

Activity   Have participants change into swimsuits.

Water Activities Practice

Note: See Appendix A, Water Skills Reference
Guide for Instructors, for the steps of each
water skill to be taught and practiced in this
session. See Appendix B, Emergency Water
Safety Skills Checklist, to keep a record of
participants' progress.

Rescue Breathing in Shallow and Deep Water

**Suggested
Time**   20 minutes

Activity   Refer participants to the *Basic Water Safety*
text, page 55, and to the *Emergency Water
Safety* text, page 19.

Demonstrate the technique for rescue
breathing in shallow water.

Have participants practice rescue breathing
in shallow water. They should simulate rescue
breaths and not make mouth-to-mouth contact.

To help keep the victim's head above the
surface of the water, have participants practice
using a solid support by holding onto the dock
or edge of the pool. Have them practice
without the support so they can learn how
hard it is to keep the victim's head above
water.

Move participants and victims to deep
water and have them practice holding on to
the deck or edge of the pool. Supervise this
practice very closely.

Recovery of Submerged Victim

**Suggested
Time**   25 minutes

Activity   Refer participants to pages 14–15 of the
textbook.
   Review the methods of recovering a
submerged victim.
- Standing on land or deck, use a reaching
  device to encircle the victim's body or snag
  victim's clothing and pull the victim to the
  surface.
- If the victim cannot be seen or reached,
  determine exact location where victim went
  underwater and direct rescuers to that
  place.
- Explain how to determine a victim's
  location and illustrate the technique by
  using objects in your facility or a
  chalkboard diagram.

   To practice rescue sightings, position
participants or floating objects at various
locations to represent places where victims
submerged. Ask participants to use fixed
objects in the surroundings to practice single-
rescuer sightings and two-rescuer sightings.

Surface Diving
Explain the procedures for recovering a
submerged victim by surface diving.
   Describe the two types of surface dives:
- Feetfirst
- Pike

   Note that surface diving to recover a victim
is best done with mask and fins, if available.
The mask enhances visibility, and fins increase
speed.
   Explain that the feetfirst dive is best for
murky water or unknown water depths.

Explain and demonstrate the feetfirst
surface dive.

Explain that the pike surface dive is best for
unknown water depths.

Explain and demonstrate the pike surface
dive.

Have participants practice the feetfirst
surface dive and the pike surface dive.

Swimming Underwater
Explain and demonstrate swimming
underwater. After a surface dive, level off in a
horizontal position underwater and swim
forward.

Have participants use their most efficient
stroke. One common stroke is a modified
breaststroke: the arms pull to the thighs with a
sidestroke kick.

Have participants practice for a distance no
greater than 25 feet at first. Caution participants against hyperventilation.

Practice only in the presence of a lifeguard.

Recovery
Use a 10-pound diving brick, other weighted
objects, or a training manikin designed for
water use to simulate a victim.

Explain and demonstrate how to recover a
submerged victim by surface diving at the spot
where the victim was last seen.

Have participants practice in shoulder-deep
water and then in deeper water.

Escapes

**Suggested
Time**   20 minutes

Activity   Refer participants to pages 19–20 in the textbook.

Discuss and review the guidelines for protecting yourself while making assists, and provide an overview of escape techniques.

Have participants walk through the steps of the escapes on land while you check various parts of each skill.

Then have participants practice escapes in shallow water before going in deep water.

To ensure safety, instruct participants in the "Let Go!" signal. Partners must agree before going into water whether their "Let Go!" signal will be three pinches or three taps.

Discuss, demonstrate, and have participants practice the following escapes:

- **Blocking**
- **Submerging**
- **Front Head-Hold Escape**
- **Rear Head-Hold Escape**
- **Wrist/Arm Escape**

Removal From Water

Suggested Time
20 minutes

Activity
Explain and demonstrate methods of removing victims from the water and discuss general guidelines.

- A **shallow water assist** is used for a swimmer who needs some support walking.
- A **drag assist** is used at a sloping beach. It is particularly useful for heavy victims.
- The **lift** is used when it is necessary to get a victim out of the water and onto a dock or pier. Do not use the lift for victims of suspected spinal injury.

Have participants practice on partners of varying sizes and weights.

End of Emergency Water Safety Session 2

Emergency Water Safety—Session 3

Lesson Plan

Suggested Time 3 hours

Topics Spinal injury management; skills test and written test; course evaluation; mask, snorkel, and fins (optional).

Equipment
- *Emergency Water Safety* textbook, 1 per participant
- Audiovisual: *Spinal Injury Management*
- Backboard, 1 for every 5 participants
- Rigid cervical collar, 1 for every backboard
- Velcro straps, cravats, or ties for use with backboard
- Pencils
- Written tests and answer sheets (photocopy from Appendix G), 1 each per participant
- Mask, snorkel, and fins, 1 set per 1 to 3 participants (optional)
- Optional audiovisual: American Red Cross *Snorkeling Skills and Rescue Techniques*
- Mask-defogging solution (optional)

Facilities Classroom, deck, or land for group discussions; pool, lake, or other swimming facility for water activities.

Objectives At the end of this session, participants will be able to describe the signs of a spinal injury and describe and demonstrate the general rescue procedures for the victim of a suspected spinal injury in the water. Specifically, they will be able to—
1. Describe the signs and symptoms of a spinal injury.

2. Describe the general rescue procedures for the victim of a suspected spinal injury in the water.
3. Provide hip and shoulder support for the victim of a suspected spinal injury.
4. Stabilize the victim of a suspected spinal injury using the head splint technique.
5. Put a victim on a backboard, apply a cervical collar, strap the victim, and remove the board from the water

Optional Objectives:
6. Identify criteria for selecting mask, snorkel, and fins.
7. Put on a mask, snorkel, and fins.
8. Clear a snorkel and mask.
9. Enter water with mask, snorkel, and fins using a sit-in entry and a stride-jump entry.
10. Swim with mask, snorkel, and fins.

Review of Session 2 and Discussion of Objectives

**Suggested
Time**   5 minutes

Activity   Select some questions from those below to
provide a review of Session 2 and a transition
into Session 3.

- What should you do if a drowning victim
  lies submerged on the bottom? What if you
  can't see or reach the victim?
- How can you protect yourself from injury
  when removing a victim from the water?
- In what situation would a drag assist be
  useful?
- In what situation would a lift be necessary?
- If, after trying, you are unable to lift a
  victim from the water at poolside, what
  should you do?
- How can you protect yourself from being
  grabbed by a panicky victim?
- Why is it important to know how to escape
  from a victim's grasp?
- What are the steps in rescue breathing?
- How do you check for responsiveness if
  the victim is not moving?
- How do you check for a pulse when you
  are giving rescue breathing to an adult?

Discuss the objectives for Session 3.

Spinal Injury

Suggested Time

35 minutes (includes 25 minutes for video)

Activity

Review with participants how to evaluate a situation and ask participants to think about the mechanism of injury that could cause a spinal injury.
- Any fall from a height greater than the victim's height
- Any person found unconscious or submerged in shallow water for unknown reasons
- Any significant head trauma
- All diving accidents

Review with participants the signs and symptoms of a possible spinal injury.
- Pain at the site of a fracture
- Loss of movement in the extremities above or below a fracture site
- Loss of feeling or tingling in the extremities
- Disorientation
- Neck or back deformity
- Visible bruising over an area of the spinal column
- Impaired breathing
- Head injury
- Fluid or blood in ears

Explain and discuss the following general procedures for handling the victim of a suspected spinal injury in the water.
- Activate facility's emergency plan.
- Approach victim carefully. Minimize water movement. Do not jump or dive into a position near victim.
- Reduce or prevent any movement of victim's spine.

- Immobilize victim's head, neck, and back. Use the hip and shoulder support technique.
- Move victim to the surface of the water, if necessary.
- Rotate victim, if necessary, to a horizontal position. Use the head splint support technique.
- Move victim to shallow water, if possible. Swim fins are helpful in keeping a victim afloat in deep water.
- Check for breathing, and maintain an open airway.
- Position the backboard under the victim.
- Secure the victim to the backboard.
- Remove the victim from the water.
- Keep the victim warm.

Optional Audiovisual: "Spinal Injury Management"

Suggested Time   25 minutes

Activity   Show the video and discuss it. (The video is optional but strongly recommended.) Explain that not all of the skills shown in the video are taught in this course because the video is also used for lifeguarding courses.

Break

**Suggested
Time** 15 minutes

Activity Have participants change into swimsuits for
water activities.

Water Activities Practice

Note: See Appendix A, Water Skills Reference
Guide for Instructors, for the steps of each
water skill to be taught and practiced in this
session. See Appendix B, Emergency Water
Safety Skills Checklist, to keep a record of
participants' progress.

Spinal Injury Management

Suggested Time   60 minutes

Activity

Hip and Shoulder Support

Explain that this technique is used only in calm, shallow water for a faceup victim of suspected spinal injury when no help is immediately available to assist in boarding (placing the victim on a backboard).

- Demonstrate hip and shoulder support in shallow water.
- Have participants practice with partners in shallow water.

Head Splint

Explain that this technique is for calm or choppy water, deep or shallow, for a facedown victim. Use the head split to turn the victim faceup.

- Explain and demonstrate the head splint.

Head/Chin Support

Explain that this technique is used in any type or condition of water for faceup or facedown victims.

- Explain and demonstrate the head/chin support technique.
- Have participants practice the head/chin support technique in shallow water.

Boarding Procedures

Explain that these techniques are for moving a victim onto a backboard after stabilization.

- Explain and demonstrate boarding procedures.
- Have participants practice this procedure with a minimum of four people, one at the head and three around the board. Another person takes the part of the victim.

Removal From Water

Demonstrate and explain the steps for removing the backboard from the water to a pool deck or dock.

- Remind participants that the rescuer at the victim's head gives directions.
- Have participants practice removing a boarded spinal injury victim from the water.

Skills Test

Suggested Time

35 minutes

Activity

Explain the testing procedures. Remind participants that all skills must be performed satisfactorily in order for the participant to pass the test and the course. Use the space provided under "Final Tests" in the Emergency Water Safety Skills Checklist in Appendix B to check off the test skills as the participants satisfactorily complete them.

Participants must successfully perform all of the skills listed below:
1. Stride jump to a passive victim in deep water. Using a single armpit tow, return the victim to the side or dock.
2. Ease into shallow water, swim to a passive victim, perform a wrist tow, return to shallow water, and position victim for rescue breathing.
3. Enter the water, perform a feetfirst or a pike surface dive, retrieve brick in 6 to 8 feet of water and bring it to the surface.
4. Perform the hip and shoulder support technique.

Written Test

Suggested Time   20 minutes

Activity   Hand out the written tests and answer sheets from Appendix G. Make sure you have made 1 copy of each for each participant.

- Tell the participants not to use their texts, notes, or talk to other participants when taking the test.
- Give participants 20 minutes to complete the test.
- Have them return the tests and answer sheets to you.
- Correct the test using the answer key in Appendix G.
- While you are correcting the tests, have participants complete the Participant Evaluation found in Appendix E, or another evaluation used by your Red Cross chapter or unit.

Evaluation, Administration, and Wrap-Up

Suggested Time

10 minutes

Activity

Review with participants the Emergency Water Safety course objectives and how they have been met. Encourage participants to continue their training by taking other American Red Cross water safety courses.

Issue or mail an *American Red Cross Emergency Water Safety Course Completion Certificate* (Cert. 3413) to participants who score 80 percent or better on the written test and who demonstrated proficiency in all the required skills.

Complete the *Course Record* (Form 6418) and return it to your local Red Cross unit with the Participant Evaluations. Remember when you teach this course the first and fourth times to fill out the Instructor Evaluation and send it to the Red Cross national headquarters.

**End of Emergency Water Safety Session 3
(The next part of the course is optional)**

Optional Session
Mask, Fins, and Snorkel

Suggested Time

1 hour, 10 minutes for the complete optional section

Equipment

- *Emergency Water Safety* textbook, 1 per participant
- Mask, fins, and snorkel, 1 set for every 1 to 3 participants
- Optional audiovisual: *Snorkeling Skills and Rescue Techniques* (13 minutes)
- Mask-defogging solution

Objectives

At the end of this session, participants will be able to—
1. Identify criteria for selecting mask, fins, and snorkel.
2. Put on mask, fins, and snorkel properly.
3. Clear snorkel and mask.
4. Enter water with mask and snorkel using a sit-in entry.
5. Enter water using a stride-jump entry wearing mask, fins, and snorkel.
6. Swim with mask, fins, and snorkel.

Activity

Discuss (15 minutes) or show *Snorkeling Skills and Rescue Techniques* audiovisual (13 minutes). Point out that mask, fins, and snorkel can be used for added swimming enjoyment, underwater exploration, rescue, and recovery.

Emphasize that swimming with this equipment requires knowledge of each piece of equipment, an understanding of safety guidelines, and plenty of practice. Point out that using the equipment properly and safely will add to swimming enjoyment and help prevent injury.

Discuss the advantage of using mask, fins, and snorkel in rescues.
- Help in swimming
- Speed in getting to victim
- Conservation of energy
- Additional power to tow victim or recover submerged victim
- Help in keeping suspected spinal injury victim horizontal in deep water
- Help in locating victim underwater

Review the safety tips (pages 49–50 of the text) for using mask, fins, and snorkel. Ask participants to explain why each one is important.

Break

**Suggested
Time** 10 minutes

Activity Participants should change clothes and prepare
for the water activities.

Water Activities Practice

Note: See Appendix A, Water Skills Reference
Guide for Instructors, for the steps of each
water skill to be taught and practiced in this
session. See Appendix B, Emergency Water
Safety Skills Checklist, to keep a record of
participant's progress.

Mask and Snorkel

Suggested Time

10 minutes

Activity

Refer participants to pages 51–53 and 56–57 in the textbook.

Display a swim mask and point out its features. Note the importance of proper fit.

Demonstrate how to test a mask for proper fit and have participants test theirs.

Check each participant's mask to be sure of proper fit.

Demonstrate and have participants practice defogging and putting on a mask.

In shallow water, demonstrate and have participants practice clearing a mask in an upright position or in a horizontal position.

Explain that mask and ear pressure can result from deep diving and can cause pain and possible injury.

Demonstrate and have participants practice equalizing mask pressure.

Discuss the function and features of a snorkel, using one or more snorkels for illustration. Demonstrate and have participants practice putting on and breathing through a snorkel in chest-deep water.

Explain that getting water in the snorkel is common, both from diving and from splashing at the surface.

Demonstrate and have participants practice flooding and emptying a snorkel in chest-deep water.

Fins

Suggested Time

10 minutes

Activity

Refer participants to pages 53–55 in the textbook.

Discuss types of fins and proper fit, using a pair of fins for illustration. Demonstrate and have participants practice putting on and walking backwards with fins on land and in water.

Demonstrate and have participants practice a modified flutter kick with fins.

Demonstrate and have participants practice the dolphin kick with fins. Tell them to keep fins underwater to maximize propulsion.

Water Entries with Equipment

Suggested Time

10 minutes

Activity

Refer participants to pages 57–59 in the textbook.

Discuss how to enter the water wearing a mask, snorkel, and fins. Explain that the sit-in entry can be done safely from a height no greater than one foot above the water.

Demonstrate without fins a sit-in entry from a low surface.

Explain and demonstrate the stride-jump entry.

Have participants practice the sit-in entry without fins and the stride-jump entry with fins.

Swimming with Equipment

**Suggested
Time**   15 minutes

Activity   Refer participants to pages 58–59 in the
textbook.
   Demonstrate swimming with equipment.
   Demonstrate a pike surface dive, swim, and
resurface using mask, fins, and snorkel.
   Have participants practice the following
routine:
1. Enter water.
2. Swim to designated point.
3. Do pike surface dive.
4. Return to surface.
5. Swim back to starting point.

   Using a weighted object as the victim,
review, demonstrate, and have the participants
practice the procedures for recovering a
submerged victim by surface diving.
Review tows and have participants practice
towing a victim.
   Review and summarize the key points of
this session by asking some of the following
questions:
- Why is it important to swim with
  companions?
- How can you check for proper fit of a
  mask?
- What is in a full set of equipment for diving
  in open water areas?
- What is the purpose of clearing a mask?
- What should you do if your snorkel floods?
- What precautions should you take before
  resurfacing?

   Since this section is optional, you will not
need to test participants on its content.

Appendix A

Water Skills Reference Guide for Instructors

Basic Water Safety Skills
Emergency Water Safety Skills

Water Skills Reference Guide for Instructors

Basic Water Safety Skills

This Water Skills Reference Guide has been prepared for instructors to use at the pool or waterfront facility. It should be pulled out of this instructor's manual and used to check the steps and the sequence of the water skills as the participants complete them.

Session 1

Facedown (Survival) Floating

1. In a near-vertical position, take a breath.
2. Put face in water, relax arms and legs, rest 2-3 seconds with the back of head at or just below surface.
3. Slowly lift arms to shoulder height, separate legs in scissors or stride-type motion.
4. Exhale while tilting head up and back.
5. To bring mouth above surface, slowly press arms downward and bring legs together. Inhale and repeat sequence.

Backfloat with Winging and Kicking

1. Start from a floating position on back.
2. Draw hands up side of body to lower ribs, extend fingers and hands outward, push hands in circular motion toward feet.
3. Add an easy flutter kick for balance, if needed.

Treading Water

1. Start from vertical position.
2. Add wide sculling motion.
3. Add easy, efficient kick (i.e., bicycle, scissors, or breaststroke).

Bobbing

1. Take deep breath in shallow water.
2. Submerge to bottom (if standing, keep feet on bottom and bend knees).
3. Push off bottom towards safety, at forward angle.
4. Exhale as you surface; repeat sequence.

Leg Cramp Release

1. From near-vertical position, take a breath.
2. Roll facedown.
3. Extend cramped leg and flex foot (push heel towards bottom, point toe towards head).
4. Knead or massage muscle.

Basic Water Safety Skills

Session 2

Spinal Injury

Hip and Shoulder Support

1. Stand facing victim's side, lower self to chest depth.
2. Slide one arm under the shoulders and other under the hip bones to support the victim.
3. Do not lift victim. Maintain victim in a horizontal position in the water until help arrives.

Assists

Reaching Assists From Land

1. Brace self to ensure balance and secure footing.
2. Extend any object that will reach the person.
3. Tell victim to grab object.
4. Pull victim carefully to safety.

Reaching Assists From Water

1. Grasp secure object at water's edge.
2. Slip into water.
3. Maintain grasp and extend free hand, leg, or rescue device. (When grasping with free hand, don't allow victim to grab you.)
4. Pull victim towards safety.

Throwing Assists

1. Assume balanced stance, foot back on throwing-hand side, other foot forward and stepping on end of line (rope).
2. Hold half the coiled line in throwing hand, other half over open palm of other hand.
3. Throw underhand, let line uncoil freely.
4. Aim just beyond victim's shoulder.

5. When victim grasps line, stand sideways, lean away from victim, and slowly pull in.

Wading Assists With Flotation Device

1. Wade in with device in front of you, checking water for hazards visually and with feet.
2. Have victim grasp other side of device and slowly pull victim to safety.

Wading Assists With Free-Floating Support

1. Wade in with support in front of you, checking water for hazards visually and with feet.
2. Push support so it floats out to victim.
3. Encourage victim to grasp the support and kick toward safety.

Using Clothes for Flotation

Blowing Air
1. Tuck in shirttail. Button shirt, leaving second and third buttons down from neck open. Keep shirt under water.
2. Lean head back, take a breath.
3. Bend head forward, blow into shirt.

Splashing Air
1. Button shirt so neck of shirt is snug to body.
2. Float on back. With one hand, hold shirttail under water; with other hand, splash air under shirttail.
3. Let air bubbles rise to shoulders.
4. Lift feet and float, repeat step 2 as necessary.

Basic Water Safety Skills

Session 3

H.E.L.P. Position

1. In a vertical position, wearing a PFD, draw knees up to chest.
2. Hold upper arms at sides; fold lower part of arms around chest.

Huddle Position (for two or more persons)

1. In a vertical position, wearing a PFD, wrap arms around each other's shoulders.
2. Keep sides of chests together, and sandwich any children between adults.

Opening Airway and Positioning for Rescue Breathing in Shallow Water

1. Check for unresponsiveness.
2. Shout for help.
3. Position the victim.
   —Stand facing victim's side between victim's shoulders and waist, with victim's head to your left.
   —Support victim by sliding your right hand between victim's right arm and side, and across upper back.
   —Place your left hand on the victim's forehead and open the airway by tilting the head back.
4. Check for breathing: look, listen, and feel.
5. Support victim with a supporting device (rescue tube, ring buoy, edge of pool) in your right hand.

Boating Safety

Trimming a Boat

1. Distribute weight evenly (front-to-back and side-to-side).
2. Stay within weight capacity of craft.
3. Keep boat trimmed (balanced) with every movement.

Boarding and Debarking a Boat

1. With boat tied to dock, make sure boat is steady.
2. Board or debark near center of craft from dock, over bow or stern from beach; keep weight low.
3. Board or debark with one foot at a time, grasping gunwale; keep weight low.

Changing Positions

1. Only one person moves at a time.
2. Keep weight low, near center of boat, and keep boat trimmed (balanced).

Using Capsized Boat for Flotation

1. Stay with the boat.
2. With one person, hold onto hull of boat or bow/stern of boat.
3. With two or more persons, balance on opposite sides of boat, grab wrists across keel.

Reentering and Paddling a Swamped Boat

1. Stay with the boat.
2. People move to opposite sides of the boat before reentering.
3. Reach over gunwale; place hands in bottom.
4. Kick feet to surface.
5. Roll over and sit in bottom of boat; hand-paddle.

Reaching and Throwing Assists From Boat

1. Approach victim against wind or current. Turn off motor 3 boat lengths from victim.
2. Throw a flotation device with line attached and tow victim to boat. Also use oar, towel, or hand to assist victim to boat.
3. Keep boat trimmed. Have passengers move to the area of the boat opposite where the victim is coming aboard.

Helping Victim Get Aboard

1. Keep boat trimmed. Have passengers move to the area of the boat opposite where the victim is coming aboard.
2. One passenger helps victim out of the water.
3. Keeping weight low and using legs, not back, "jackknife" victim at waist over side of boat and swing victim's legs into boat.

Emergency Water Safety Skills

Session 1

Human Chain

1. Anchor (first rescuer) holds onto a secure object on land with one hand.
2. With the other hand, anchor grabs second rescuer (who is facing opposite way) wrist-to-wrist.
3. Second rescuer grabs third (facing opposite way), wrist-to-wrist, and so on.
4. Lightest person is farthest out, and extends reach with long object, if necessary.
5. Everyone leans back toward shore, and anchor person pulls in second, who pulls in third, and so on.

Water Entries

Stride-Jump Entry

1. Stand with shoulders forward of hips, arms extended forward or to sides just above shoulder height.
2. Leap forward into water, one leg forward and the other back.
3. On entering water, press hands down, squeeze legs together to keep head above water.

Feetfirst-Jump Entry

1. Jump with head erect, eyes on victim.
2. On entering water, spread arms and legs to stop descent.
3. Come to surface and begin stroking toward victim.

Positioning (Ready Position)

1. With flotation device, get to passive victim quickly.
2. Stop just short of victim's reach.
3. Tuck legs under body, sweep arms forward, extend device.

Tows

Wrist Tow

1. Get into position to tow passive victim.
2. Grasp underside of victim's wrist; keep towing arm straight.
3. Roll passive victim faceup if necessary.
4. Use modified sidestroke or modified elementary backstroke.
5. Keep victim's face above water.

Armpit Tow

1. Get into position to tow passive victim.
2. Roll passive victim faceup if necessary.
3. Place fingers in victim's armpit, thumb secures hold on outside of victim's upper arm. Keep towing arm straight.
4. Use strong sidestroke or modified elementary backstroke.
5. Keep victim's face above water.

Collar Tow (optional)

1. Get into position to tow passive victim.
2. Roll passive victim faceup if necessary.
3. Grasp victim's collar (or just below it if collar grasp tightens too much around victim's throat) with palm down.
4. Grasp with palm down so arm can support victim's head.
5. Keep towing arm straight.
6. Use modified sidestroke or modified elementary backstroke.
7. Keep victim's face out of the water.

Rescue Tube Tow

1. Get into position to tow victim.
2. Extend tube or ring buoy to victim; tell victim to grasp device.
3. Hold rescue tube strap or ring buoy with straight arm.
4. Use sidestroke or modified elementary backstroke.
5. Reassure victim.

Changing Positions (From Wrist Tow to Armpit Tow) (optional)

1. Continue sidestroke or elementary backstroke kick.
2. Maintaining grasp on victim's wrist, bend your elbow to pull the victim closer to you.
3. With free hand, grasp victim's armpit. Always maintain contact with the victim.
4. Release victim's wrist and continue with the armpit tow.

Emergency Water Safety Skills

Session 2

Rescue Breathing in Shallow and Deep Water

1. With victim's head to your left side, slide right arm between the victim's right arm and body and support victim's upper body.
2. For maximum support, particularly in deep water, hold onto solid support or flotation device with right hand.
3. Keep victim's head above the surface.
4. Bring free hand overhead to pinch victim's nose.
5. Begin rescue breathing.

Recovery of Submerged Victim

Feetfirst Surface Dive

1. Start by treading water.
2. Press down vigorously towards bottom with hands and simultaneously give strong kick.
3. Body is in straight, vertical position to descend.
4. When downward body momentum begins to slow, press vigorously upward, arms over head, to continue descent. Repeat this step until at desired depth.

Pike Surface Dive

1. Start from front float position.
2. Lower head and bend at the hips, while pressing arms and palms backward to thighs to gain momentum.
3. Lift legs while looking toward the bottom and bring arms over head.

4. Legs will be above surface, and their weight will force swimmer down.

Underwater Swimming
1. From a surface dive, level off underwater into horizontal position.
2. Use modified breaststroke. Continue breaststroke arm-pull back to thighs, kick, then glide with arms at sides.

Recovery
1. Perform surface dive to reach victim.
2. Grasp any part of body or clothing that allows firm hold.
3. Plant feet on bottom and push off. If bottom is too soft, kick vigorously; use free hand to pull victim to surface.

Escapes
Block
1. Take a breath, duck head.
2. Put one hand high on victim's chest, extend arm, and push victim away.
3. Swim away underwater and surface safe distance from victim.

Submerge
1. Take a breath and submerge with victim hanging on.
2. Stay under water until victim lets go.

Front Head-Hold Escape
1. Take breath, tuck and turn chin, raise shoulders and submerge.

2. Bring hands to undersides of victim's arms and push straight up extending arms to break hold.
3. When free from hold, quickly swim backwards out of reach and surface.

Rear Head-Hold Escape
1. Take a breath, tuck chin down and to the side, raise shoulders, and submerge.
2. Bring hands to undersides of victim's arms at elbows; push up straight to break hold.
3. When free from grasp, swim away backwards and surface out of victim's reach.

Wrist/Arm Escape
Wrist or lower arm
1. Take a breath, submerge, and try to pull free.
2. Grasp your own hand with free hand and pull hard.

Upper arm
1. Take a breath, submerge, and place hand of grabbed arm on victim's chest.
2. Reach across with free hand, place it on victim's head or shoulder, push victim underwater, and pull free.

Removal from Water
Shallow Water Assist
1. Tired or weak person stands at your right side.
2. Place your right hand around victim's waist.
3. Place victim's left arm around your shoulders.
4. Grasp victim's left arm and slowly assist out of the water.

Drag

1. In standing-depth water, move behind victim and grasp victim firmly in both armpits.
2. Walk backward slowly toward beach, pulling victim.
3. Use legs to absorb the weight of victim; keep back as straight as possible.

Lift from Water

1. Tow victim to edge of pier, dock, pool deck. Face victim toward edge.
2. Support victim with knee; reach under victim's armpits and grab edge.
3. Place victim's hands on top of each other on the deck. Place one hand on top of victim's hands, move to one side of the victim. Climb out of water without losing contact with victim.
4. Face victim and grasp victim's wrists.
5. Stand near edge, bend knees, and lift victim straight up until upper body clears the edge.
6. Lean back, and bring victim's torso against your forward leg to allow victim's upper body to slide gently to a facedown position on deck. Protect victim's head.
7. Place one hand on victim's shoulder, grasp one thigh with free hand, and swing both of victim's legs onto deck.

Emergency Water Safety Skills

Session 3

Spinal Injury Skills
Hip and Shoulder Support
1. Stand facing victim's side; lower yourself to chest depth.
2. Slide one arm under the shoulders and other under the hip bones to support the victim.
3. Do not lift victim. Maintain victim in a horizontal position in the water until help arrives.

Head Splint Technique
1. Stand facing victim's side; lower yourself to chest depth.
2. Gently float victim's arms up alongside the head, parallel to surface. Grasp the victim's arms midway between the shoulder and elbow. With your right hand, grasp victim's right arm. With your left hand, grasp victim's left arm. Extend victim's arms against victim's head.
3. Apply pressure to the arms to splint the head.
4. Lower yourself to chest depth. Glide victim's body to surface.
5. With victim horizontal in water, continue moving and rotate victim. Push victim's arm that is closer to you underwater and pull victim's other arm across surface to turn victim faceup. Lower your shoulders into the water.
6. Rest victim's head in crook of your arm, but not on your arm.
7. Maintain victim in horizontal position in the water until help arrives.

Head/Chin Support

1. Approach victim from either side. Position victim's nearer arm along victim's side.
2. Lower your body until shoulders are at water level.
3. Place your forearms along length of victim's breastbone and spine.
4. Use your top hand to support the victim's chin, thumb on one side, fingers on the other. The bottom hand supports the victim's head at the base of the skull, but does not apply pressure yet.
5. Lock both wrists and squeeze forearms together to clamp victim's chest and back between them. Support chin and base of skull.
6. Glide victim to horizontal position. If victim is facedown, turn victim faceup.
7. To turn victim faceup, slowly rotate victim towards you. Submerge, and carefully go under victim as you rotate the victim to other side.
8. Maintain victim in horizontal position until help arrives.

Boarding Procedures

1. The person stabilizing the victim's head and neck directs others to assist in placing backboard and securing victim.
2. Bring backboard into water; approach victim from side.
3. Place backboard diagonally under victim from the side (the foot end goes in water first).
4. Hold board underwater. Slide board under victim and position it lengthwise along victim's spine. The board should be several inches beyond victim's head.
5. Allow board to rise under victim with at least one rescuer on each side of board, and one at victim's feet.
6. Person providing stabilization carefully withdraws hands. Second rescuer maintains in-line stabilization.

7. First rescuer places cervical collar on victim. Collar must fit securely, chin in proper resting position and head maintained in neutral position by collar.
8. Once collar is in place, secure victim to backboard using straps or cravats.
9. Criss-cross chest and secure at the sides.
10. Secure hips.
11. Secure hands in front of victim.
12. Secure thighs and shins.
13. Pad any void between back of head and backboard to keep head in neutral position.
14. Secure head by placing towel roll in horseshoe shape around head and neck of victim.
15. Secure head with cravats.

Removal From Water
1. Rescuer at victim's head directs the action.
2. If in a pool, move board perpendicular to side of pool.
3. Keep board horizontal during removal.
4. Two people must be on the deck to help lift and slide board onto deck or dock.
5. Remove board headfirst.

Emergency Water Safety Skills

Optional Session 3

Mask, Fins, and Snorkel

Clearing Mask

1. In shallow water, submerge and flood mask by briefly lifting an edge or pulling mask away from face.
2. From vertical position, place palms across top of mask and firmly apply pressure against forehead. Tilt head back and exhale forcefully through nose, forcing water out bottom of mask.
3. From facedown horizontal position , turn head to one side, apply firm pressure on high side of mask, exhale forcefully through nose, forcing water out bottom of mask.

Equalizing Pressure (Mask and Ear)

1. Mask pressure: Submerge and exhale through your nose.
2. Ear pressure: Place your thumb against bottom of mask, press mask against face, and exhale through nose. Swallow and move your jaws.

Sit-In Entry

1. Stand at edge of pool with back towards water, heels at edge.
2. Hold mask and snorkel securely against face with one hand. Keep elbow against ribs, other arm extended down by side.
3. Tuck chin and bend into sitting position; lean back and sit in water.

Stride-Jump Entry

1. Hold mask firmly in place with one hand covering faceplate and elbow close to chest, other arm extended down by side.
2. Step out with a long stride over water leaning slightly forward.
3. When fins touch water, bring legs together with toes pointed.
4. Keep head and shoulders above water.

Appendix B

Water Safety Skills Checklists

Basic Water Safety Skills Checklist
Emergency Water Safety Skills Checklist

American Red Cross

**BASIC WATER SAFETY
SKILLS CHECKLIST**

		Names
Level of Participation	Observer (O)	
	PFD-Wearer (PFD)	
	Swimmer (S)	
Sudden Immersion Skills	Survival Floating	
	Back Float with Winging and Kick	
	Treading Water	
	Bobbing	
	Cramp Release	
	Clothing—Swimming	
	Clothing—Inflating	
Spinal Injury	Hip and Shoulder Support	
Assists	Reaching—Out-of-Water	
	Reaching—In-Water	
	Throwing	
	Wading	
PFDs	H.E.L.P Position	
	Huddle Position	
Rescue Breathing	Opening Airway—on Land	
	Opening Airway—in Shallow Water	
Boating Safety	Trimming	
	Change Positions	
	Use Overturned Boat for Flotation	
	Reenter and Paddle Swamped Boat	
	Assists	

Checklists are not to be sent to chapter. Retain for own use.

American Red Cross

EMERGENCY WATER SAFETY

SKILLS CHECKLIST

Check off the skills listed on the left in the boxes that are shaded **gray**.

Check off the skills listed on the right in the **unshaded** boxes.

Names

Left-side skill categories and skills:

- **Assist**
  - Human Chain
- **Entries**
  - Stride Jump
  - Feetfirst Jump
- **Tows**
  - Positioning
  - Rescue Tube
  - Wrist
  - Armpit
  - Collar
  - Changing Positions
- **Recovery of Submerged Victim**
  - Feetfirst Surface Dive
  - Pike Surface Dive
  - Underwater Swimming
  - Recovery
- **Escapes**
  - Block
  - Front Head-Hold
  - Rear Head-Hold
  - Wrist/Arm

Top skill categories and skills:

- **Removal From Water**
  - Shallow Water Assist
  - Drag
  - Lift
- **Spinal Injury Management**
  - Hip and Shoulder Support
  - Head Splint
  - Head/Chin Support
  - Boarding Procedures
  - Removal From Water
- **Rescue Breathing**
  - Shallow Water
  - Deep Water
- **Mask, Fins, Snorkel**
  - Clearing and Relieving Pressure
  - Sit-in Entry
  - Stride-Jump Entry
  - Swimming
- **Final Tests**
  - Written
  - Skill 1
  - Skill 2
  - Skill 3
  - Skill 4

Checklists are not to be sent to chapter. Retain for own use.

Appendix C

Equipment and Supplies

Basic Water Safety
Emergency Water Safety

Equipment and Supplies

Basic Water Safety

Supplies Required for Participants

- ☐ *American Red Cross Basic Water Safety* textbook (Stock No. 329312)
- ☐ Wearable PFDs in good condition, 1 per participant
- ☐ Clothing to wear in water: long-sleeved shirts and pants
- ☐ Notebook and pen or pencil
- ☐ Swimsuit and towel for every session
- ☐ Participant Course Evaluation
- ☐ _____
- ☐ _____

Equipment Required for the Course

- ☐ Enrollment and registration materials
- ☐ Water Skills Reference Guide for Instructors (Appendix A)
- ☐ Basic Water Safety Skills Checklist (Appendix B)
- ☐ *American Red Cross Rescue Breathing and Choking Supplement* (Stock No. 329286)
- ☐ Chalkboard and chalk or flip chart and markers
- ☐ Video projection equipment and spare parts
- ☐ 5 different types of PFDs for display
- ☐ Rescue tubes and ring buoys, 1 for every 3 to 4 participants
- ☐ Shepherd's crook
- ☐ Heaving line
- ☐ Throw bag
- ☐ Improvised reaching assist equipment
- ☐ Instructor Course Evaluation for first and fourth teaching
- ☐ **Recommended video**
  - ☐ *Spinal Injury Management* (Stock No. 329328) 25 minutes
- ☐ **Boating Safety Equipment**
  - ☐ Sound-signaling device—whistle, horn, or bell
  - ☐ Visual distress signaling devices—flares or flags for daytime, flares or electric lights for nighttime
  - ☐ Anchor
  - ☐ Extra line
  - ☐ Throw bag

(Basic Water Safety continued)

- ❑ First aid kit
- ❑ Bailing device
- ❑ Copies of federal, state, and local boating regulations
- ❑ One or more small craft (under 16 feet in length) such as a row boat or canoe (optional)
- ❑ **Optional audiovisuals**
  - ❑ *Survival Swimming* (Stock No. 321649) 8 minutes
  - ❑ *Boating Safety and Rescues* (Stock No. 321656) 11 minutes
  - ❑ *Nonswimming Rescues* (Stock No. 321650) 8 minutes
- ❑ _____
- ❑ _____

Equipment and Supplies

Emergency Water Safety

Supplies Required for Participants

- ❑ *American Red Cross Basic Water Safety* textbook (Stock No. 329312)
- ❑ *American Red Cross Emergency Water Safety* textbook (Stock No. 329313)
- ❑ *American Red Cross Rescue Breathing and Choking Supplement* (Stock No. 329268)
- ❑ Notebook and pen or pencil
- ❑ Swimsuit and towel for every session
- ❑ Participant Course Evaluation
- ❑ _____
- ❑ _____

Equipment Required for the Course

- ❑ Enrollment and registration materials
- ❑ Water Skills Reference Guide for Instructors (Appendix A)
- ❑ Emergency Water Safety Skills Checklist (Appendix B)
- ❑ Chalkboard and chalk or flip chart and markers
- ❑ 5 different types of PFDs for display
- ❑ 10-pound diving brick
- ❑ Adult manikins, 1 for every 2 to 3 participants
- ❑ Extra manikin lungs if appropriate
- ❑ Manikin decontamination solution: one-quarter cup liquid household chlorine bleach per gallon of tap water. The solution must be made fresh just prior to each class and discarded after use.
- ❑ Clean gauze pads (4" x 4"), a baby bottle brush, soap and water, basins or buckets, nonsterile disposable gloves, and other supplies recommended by the manufacturer
- ❑ Backboard, 1 for every 5 participants
- ❑ Rigid cervical collar, 1 for every backboard
- ❑ Velcro straps, cravats, or ties for use with backboard
- ❑ Written tests, 1 per participant
- ❑ Answer sheets, 1 per participant
- ❑ Mask, fins, and snorkel (optional), 1 set per every 2 to 3 participants
- ❑ Mask-defogging solution (optional)

(Emergency Water Safety Continued)

❑ **Recommended videos**
  ❑ Rescue Breathing segment of *Adult CPR* (Stock No. 329130)
    or of *Community CPR* (Stock No. 329371) 10 minutes
  ❑ *Spinal Injury Management* (Stock No. 329328)
❑ Video projection equipment and spare parts
❑ **Optional audiovisuals**
  ❑ *Snorkeling Skills and Rescue Techniques* (Stock No. 321648)
    13 minutes

❑ _____

❑ _____

Appendix D

Additional References

Additional References

Audiovisuals

Drowning Facts and Myths (1977) 10 minutes
On Drowning (1970) 17 minutes
The Reason People Drown (1988) 25 minutes
Available for purchase from:
Water Safety, Inc.
3 Boulder Brae Lane
Larchmont, New York 10538
(914) 834-7536

The Drowning Machine (1981) 20 minutes
Available for purchase from:
Hornbein Productions
740 Elmwood St.
State College, PA 16801
(814) 234-7886

Instructor References

- *American Red Cross: Adult CPR* (Stock No. 329128)
- *American Red Cross CPR Instructor's Manual*
  (Stock No. 329367)
- *American Red Cross CPR: Basic Life Support for the Professional Rescuer* (Stock No. 329365)
- *American Red Cross Standard First Aid* (Stock No. 329380)
- *American Red Cross Standard First Aid Instructor's Manual* (Stock No. 329381)
- *American Red Cross Instructor Candidate's Manual for the Introduction to Health Services Education* (Stock No. 321252)
- *Lifeguard Training* (Stock No. 321119)
- *Lifeguard Training Supplement* (Stock No. 329448)
- *Lifeguard Training Instructor's Manual* (Stock No. 329447)
- *American Red Cross Swimming and Aquatics Safety* (Stock No. 321133)

Participant Course Evaluation for Basic Water Safety and Emergency Water Safety

Same for all courses

Included here are samples of Participant Course Evaluations that you may use to find out what participants thought of the course.

By asking participants to complete an evaluation, you can learn more about how well you teach and how well course materials are meeting the participants' needs. This evaluation also reminds participants that the Red Cross is continually trying to improve its courses.

You should talk with health and safety personnel at your Red Cross chapter or unit to find out if they want you to use this form or an alternative. Follow their instructions for returning the completed forms. If your chapter or unit does not require an evaluation, you may want to use this form for your own information to help you improve your teaching.

How to Use the Participant Course Evaluation

Ask participants to fill out the Participant Course Evaluation at the end of the course. Tell participants that they do not have to identify themselves on the evaluation. To make responses confidential, ask the participants to leave the completed evaluation in a box or envelope which you have placed nearby.

American Red Cross Basic Water Safety
Participant Course Evaluation

We would like to know what you thought about this American Red Cross Basic Water Safety course. You can help maintain the high quality of the course by completing this evaluation.

Date:_____ Instructor:_____

1. Tell us what you thought of the course. (Circle or check your choice.)

	Strongly Agree	Agree	Not Sure	Don't Agree	Strongly Disagree	Did Not Use
a. The textbook explained things clearly.	1	2	3	4	5	❑
b. The videos helped me understand how I could use my skills in an emergency.	1	2	3	4	5	❑
c. The demonstrations in the videos were clear and helpful.	1	2	3	4	5	❑
d. I have confidence that I can do these skills correctly.	1	2	3	4	5	❑
e. The instructor was well prepared.	1	2	3	4	5	❑
f. The instructor answered questions clearly.	1	2	3	4	5	❑
g. The instructor helped me during the practice sessions.	1	2	3	4	5	❑
h. I would recommend this course.	1	2	3	4	5	❑
i. I know when to use the skills I learned in this course.	1	2	3	4	5	❑
j. I had to work hard to pass this course.	1	2	3	4	5	❑

2. Was all the equipment in good order? ❑ Yes ❑ No

3. Was the classroom clean and comfortable? ❑ Yes ❑ No

4. Was the pool facility clean and well-maintained? ❑ Yes ❑ No

5. Did you have enough time to read? ❑ Yes ❑ No

6. Did you have enough time to practice? ❑ Yes ❑ No

7. Did you learn what you wanted to learn? ❑ Yes ❑ No

   If yes, please specify:

If no, list what else you wanted to learn:

_____

_____

_____

8. What was your age at your last birthday? _____

9. Please check the highest level of education you have completed.
    - ❑ Elementary school ❑ Junior high school ❑ High school
    - ❑ Some college ❑ College degree or beyond

10. Check one:
    - ❑ Male
    - ❑ Female

11. Check your level of participation in this course:
    - ❑ Observer
    - ❑ PFD-wearer
    - ❑ Swimmer

12. Do you have any other comments about this course or your instructor that you would like to share with us?

_____

_____

_____

_____

_____

_____

Thank you for answering these questions. We hope you enjoyed the course.

American Red Cross Emergency Water Safety
Participant Course Evaluation

We would like to know what you thought about this American Red Cross Emergency Water Safety course. You can help maintain the high quality of the course by completing this evaluation.

Date:_____ Instructor:_____

1. Tell us what you thought of the course. (Circle or check your choice.)

	Strongly Agree	Agree	Not Sure	Don't Agree	Strongly Disagree	Did Not Use
a. The textbook explained things clearly.	1	2	3	4	5	❑
b. The videos helped me understand how I could use my skills in an emergency.	1	2	3	4	5	❑
c. The demonstrations in the videos were clear and helpful.	1	2	3	4	5	❑
d. I have confidence that I can do these skills correctly.	1	2	3	4	5	❑
e. The instructor was well prepared.	1	2	3	4	5	❑
f. The instructor answered questions clearly.	1	2	3	4	5	❑
g. The instructor helped me during the practice sessions.	1	2	3	4	5	❑
h. I would recommend this course.	1	2	3	4	5	❑
i. I know when to use the skills I learned in this course.	1	2	3	4	5	❑
j. I had to work hard to pass this course.	1	2	3	4	5	❑

2. Was all the equipment in good order?   ❑ Yes   ❑ No

3. Was the classroom clean and comfortable?   ❑ Yes   ❑ No

4. Was the pool facility clean and well-maintained?   ❑ Yes   ❑ No

5. Did you have enough time to read?   ❑ Yes   ❑ No

6. Did you have enough time to practice?   ❑ Yes   ❑ No

7. Did you learn what you wanted to learn?   ❑ Yes   ❑ No

   If yes, please specify:

If no, list what else you wanted to learn:

_____

_____

_____

8. What was your age at your last birthday? _____

9. Please check the highest level of education you have completed.
    ❑ Elementary school ❑ Junior high school ❑ High school
    ❑ Some college ❑ College degree or beyond

10. Check one:
    ❑ Male
    ❑ Female

11. Do you have any other comments about this course or your instructor that you would like to share with us?

_____

_____

_____

_____

_____

_____

Thank you for answering these questions. We hope you enjoyed the course.

Instructor Course Evaluation

This Appendix contains four copies of the Instructor Course
Evaluation. This is for your convenience in filling out the evaluations
after the first and fourth times you teach either course.

Instructor Course Evaluation

To continue to improve aquatic courses, the American Red Cross needs your help. Please complete a copy of this form the **FIRST** time you teach a Basic Water Safety or an Emergency Water Safety course, and complete another copy the **FOURTH** time you teach it. Return the completed evaluations to:

> American Red Cross
> National Headquarters
> Health and Safety
> 17th and D Streets, N.W.
> Washington, DC 20006

Background

1. Today's date: _____

2. Number of participants:_____

3. Course taught: ❑ Basic Water Safety ❑ Emergency Water Safety

4. Is this your first or fourth time teaching the course?
   ❑ First ❑ Fourth

5. What type of instructor are you?
   ❑ Red Cross volunteer
   ❑ Red Cross paid instructor
   ❑ Other (please specify): _____

6. Total time required to complete the course: ____hours, ____minutes.

7. How would you describe the participants in this course?
   ❑ Mostly under age 18   ❑ Mostly ages 18 to 40
   ❑ Mostly ages 41 to 65   ❑ Mixed ages

8. In what setting did you teach the course?
   ❑ Public Facility   ❑ School   ❑ Private Facility
   ❑ Other (describe) _____

9. How long have you been an American Red Cross Water Safety instructor? _____

10. Please list the videos or films you used when you taught this course.
    Session 1 _____
    Session 2 _____
    Session 3 _____
    Other   _____

11. Do you have any questions about the course that are not answered in the instructor's manual?

12. Do you have any suggestions for improving the instructor's manual?

13. Do you have any suggestions for improving the textbook?

14. Do you have any suggestions for improving the videos?

Optional: If you are willing to discuss your comments with us, please give us your name and a daytime phone number. We would like to be able to call you if we have any questions.

Name: _____ Phone number: (_____)_____

Red Cross chapter name:

_____

Thank you for taking the time to answer these questions. If you have any additional comments about the course, please include them on a separate sheet and attach them to this evaluation.

Instructor Course Evaluation

To continue to improve aquatic courses, the American Red Cross needs your help. Please complete a copy of this form the **FIRST** time you teach a Basic Water Safety or an Emergency Water Safety course, and complete another copy the **FOURTH** time you teach it. Return the completed evaluations to:

> American Red Cross
> National Headquarters
> Health and Safety
> 17th and D Streets, N.W.
> Washington, DC 20006

Background

1. Today's date: _____

2. Number of participants:_____

3. Course taught: ❑ Basic Water Safety   ❑ Emergency Water Safety

4. Is this your first or fourth time teaching the course?
    ❑ First   ❑ Fourth

5. What type of instructor are you?
    ❑ Red Cross volunteer
    ❑ Red Cross paid instructor
    ❑ Other (please specify): _____

6. Total time required to complete the course: ____hours, ____minutes.

7. How would you describe the participants in this course?
    ❑ Mostly under age 18   ❑ Mostly ages 18 to 40
    ❑ Mostly ages 41 to 65   ❑ Mixed ages

8. In what setting did you teach the course?
    ❑ Public Facility   ❑ School   ❑ Private Facility
    ❑ Other (describe) _____

9. How long have you been an American Red Cross Water Safety instructor? _____

10. Please list the videos or films you used when you taught this course.
    Session 1 _____
    Session 2 _____
    Session 3 _____
    Other   _____

11. Do you have any questions about the course that are not answered in the instructor's manual?

12. Do you have any suggestions for improving the instructor's manual?

13. Do you have any suggestions for improving the textbook?

14. Do you have any suggestions for improving the videos?

Optional: If you are willing to discuss your comments with us, please give us your name and a daytime phone number. We would like to be able to call you if we have any questions.

Name: _____ Phone number: (_____) _____

Red Cross chapter name:

_____

Thank you for taking the time to answer these questions. If you have any additional comments about the course, please include them on a separate sheet and attach them to this evaluation.

Instructor Course Evaluation

To continue to improve aquatic courses, the American Red Cross needs your help. Please complete a copy of this form the **FIRST** time you teach a Basic Water Safety or an Emergency Water Safety course, and complete another copy the **FOURTH** time you teach it. Return the completed evaluations to:

> American Red Cross
> National Headquarters
> Health and Safety
> 17th and D Streets, N.W.
> Washington, DC 20006

Background

1. Today's date: _____

2. Number of participants: _____

3. Course taught: ❑ Basic Water Safety ❑ Emergency Water Safety

4. Is this your first or fourth time teaching the course?
   ❑ First   ❑ Fourth

5. What type of instructor are you?
   ❑ Red Cross volunteer
   ❑ Red Cross paid instructor
   ❑ Other (please specify): _____

6. Total time required to complete the course: ____hours, ____minutes.

7. How would you describe the participants in this course?
   ❑ Mostly under age 18   ❑ Mostly ages 18 to 40
   ❑ Mostly ages 41 to 65   ❑ Mixed ages

8. In what setting did you teach the course?
   ❑ Public Facility   ❑ School   ❑ Private Facility
   ❑ Other (describe) _____

9. How long have you been an American Red Cross Water Safety instructor? _____

10. Please list the videos or films you used when you taught this course.
    Session 1 _____
    Session 2 _____
    Session 3 _____
    Other   _____

11. Do you have any questions about the course that are not answered in the instructor's manual?

12. Do you have any suggestions for improving the instructor's manual?

13. Do you have any suggestions for improving the textbook?

14. Do you have any suggestions for improving the videos?

Optional: If you are willing to discuss your comments with us, please give us your name and a daytime phone number. We would like to be able to call you if we have any questions.

Name: _____ Phone number: (_____) _____

Red Cross chapter name:

_____

Thank you for taking the time to answer these questions. If you have any additional comments about the course, please include them on a separate sheet and attach them to this evaluation.

Instructor Course Evaluation

To continue to improve aquatic courses, the American Red Cross needs your help. Please complete a copy of this form the **FIRST** time you teach a Basic Water Safety or an Emergency Water Safety course, and complete another copy the **FOURTH** time you teach it. Return the completed evaluations to:

> American Red Cross
> National Headquarters
> Health and Safety
> 17th and D Streets, N.W.
> Washington, DC 20006

Background

1. Today's date: _____

2. Number of participants:_____

3. Course taught: ☐ Basic Water Safety ☐ Emergency Water Safety

4. Is this your first or fourth time teaching the course?
   ☐ First   ☐ Fourth

5. What type of instructor are you?
   ☐ Red Cross volunteer
   ☐ Red Cross paid instructor
   ☐ Other (please specify): _____

6. Total time required to complete the course: ____hours, ____minutes.

7. How would you describe the participants in this course?
   ☐ Mostly under age 18   ☐ Mostly ages 18 to 40
   ☐ Mostly ages 41 to 65   ☐ Mixed ages

8. In what setting did you teach the course?
   ☐ Public Facility   ☐ School   ☐ Private Facility
   ☐ Other (describe) _____

9. How long have you been an American Red Cross Water Safety instructor? _____

10. Please list the videos or films you used when you taught this course.
    Session 1 _____
    Session 2 _____
    Session 3 _____
    Other   _____

11. Do you have any questions about the course that are not answered in the instructor's manual?

12. Do you have any suggestions for improving the instructor's manual?

13. Do you have any suggestions for improving the textbook?

14. Do you have any suggestions for improving the videos?

Optional: If you are willing to discuss your comments with us, please give us your name and a daytime phone number. We would like to be able to call you if we have any questions.

Name: _____ Phone number: (_____)_____

Red Cross chapter name:

_____

Thank you for taking the time to answer these questions. If you have any additional comments about the course, please include them on a separate sheet and attach them to this evaluation.

Appendix G

Emergency Water Safety
Written Test Materials

Written Test

Answer Sheet

Answer Key

(Skills Test: see page 106)

Written Test
Emergency Water Safety

IMPORTANT: Read all instructions before beginning this test.

INSTRUCTIONS: Mark all answers in pencil on the separate answer sheet. Do not write on this test. The questions on this test are multiple choice. Read each question slowly and carefully. Then choose the best answer and fill in that circle on the answer sheet. If you wish to change an answer, erase your first answer completely. Return this test to your instructor when you are finished.

1. A useful skill for water rescue is:
    a. Water skiing.
    b. Treading water.
    c. Bobbing.
    d. Butterfly stroke.

2. The difference between an active drowning victim and a passive drowning victim is:
    a. An active victim is quiet, and a passive victim shouts for help.
    b. An active victim floats on his or her back, and a passive victim treads water.
    c. An active victim struggles, and a passive victim slips under water with little or no warning.
    d. An active victim slips underwater with little or no warning, and a passive victim struggles.

3. A human chain is designed to:
    a. Be used in fast moving water.
    b. Be used in water more than waist deep.
    c. Count swimmers at a facility.
    d. Assist someone who is having difficulty in water.

4. When entering water where the depth and bottom conditions are not known, the rescuer should use the:
    a. Stride jump entry.
    b. Compact jump entry.
    c. Feet-first entry.
    d. Ease-in entry.

5. The safest way to rescue a swimmer in deep water 10 feet away is to:
    a. Make a throwing assist.
    b. Make a reaching assist with with your leg.
    c. Swim to the victim.
    d. Make a wading assist.

6. The technique of stabilizing a victim's spine is known as:
    a. Neck stabilization.
    b. Arm/head stabilization.
    c. In-line stabilization.
    d. Shoulder/head stabilization.

7. Approximately 95 percent of diving injuries occur in water that is:
    a. Over 10 feet deep.
    b. Less that 10 feet deep.
    c. Over 5 feet deep.
    d. Less than 5 feet deep.

8. Which of the following factors should influence a rescuer's actions when attempting a rescue?
   a. The location of the victim
   b. The temperature of the water
   c. Strong currents
   d. All of the above

9. Signs and symptoms of possible spinal injury include:
   a. Tingling or numbness in the extremities.
   b. Unconsciousness.
   c. Distortion of the neck.
   d. All of the above.

10. The correct sequence of rescue procedures for a victim of a suspected spinal injury is:
    a. Check for breathing, stabilization of the spine, and removal from the water.
    b. Activate the facility emergency plan, approach the victim carefully, and reduce any movement of the victim's spine.
    c. Approach the victim carefully, remove victim from the water, and check for breathing.
    d. Secure victim to a backboard, check for breathing, and keep victim warm.

11. When no immediate help is available, the simplest support in shallow water for a faceup victim of a suspected spinal injury is:
    a. Hip and foot support.
    b. Hip and shoulder support.
    c. Head and chin support.
    d. Head splint technique.

12. Use of the head/chin support technique requires the rescuer to apply pressure to the chest and spine with his or her:
    a. Hands.
    b. Wrists.
    c. Forearms.
    d. Shoulders.

13. When assessing a victim's injuries, in which situation would you suspect a spinal injury?
    a. Any fall from a height greater than the victim's height
    b. Any person found unconscious or submerged in shallow water for unknown reasons
    c. Any victim with significant head trauma
    d. All of the above

14. A properly performed wrist tow can be used:
    a. On both active and passive victims.
    b. Only on active victims.
    c. Only on passive victims.
    d. Only when an surface dive is used.

15. When lifting a victim from deep water, you should:
    a. Take care to protect the victim's head.
    b. Always maintain contact with the victim.
    c. Lift with your legs, not your back.
    d. All of the above.

16. If a distressed swimmer suddenly tries to grab you, your first reaction would be to use the:
    a. Front head-hold escape.
    b. Rear head-hold escape.
    c. Block.
    d. Wrist/arm escape.

17. If a victim grasps you firmly by the upper arm, you should:
    a. Submerge and try to swim away.
    b. Allow the victim to hang on until you get tired.
    c. Use the backstroke to swim to safety.
    d. Block the victim and use your free hand to submerge the victim.

18. The first thing you should do if you are grabbed around the head by a distressed swimmer is to:
    a. Tuck and turn your chin.
    b. Take a breath.
    c. Submerge.
    d. All of the above.

19. When entering deep water from a height of no more than 5 feet, use the:
    a. Compact jump.
    b. Pike surface dive.
    c. Ease-in entry.
    d. Feetfirst entry.

20. A ladder, flat-bottomed boat, plank, and spare car tire without a rim:
    a. Can be used to make an ice rescue.
    b. Are poor examples of ice rescue equipment.
    c. Should be used to assist a victim with possible spinal injury.
    d. Should not be used in water rescues.

21. What is the best way to open the airway of an unconscious victim?
    a. Tilt the head back and lift the chin.
    b. Tilt the head back and lift the neck.
    c. Tilt the head back and push down on the chin.
    d. Do a finger sweep followed by 6 to 10 abdominal thrusts.

22. A victim is not breathing. You give two breaths and the chest rises. What should you do next?
    a. Give two more breaths.
    b. Begin CPR.
    c. Check for a pulse.
    d. Remove water from the victim's mouth.

23. While boating, you spot a swimmer in distress. You should:
    a. Circle the victim twice before attempting a rescue.
    b. Use a reaching or throwing assist.
    c. Get to shore quickly and seek help.
    d. Leave your boat and swim to the victim.

24. The feetfirst surface dive should be used in:
    a. Murky water.
    b. Thick, grassy areas.
    c. Water of unknown depth and bottom conditions.
    d. All of the above.

25. If you see a victim go underwater as you are approaching:
    a. Surface dive in the vicinity where you last saw the victim.
    b. Go back to safety and call for help.
    c. Wait for a team of scuba divers to help.
    d. None of the above.

American Red Cross Emergency Water Safety
Answer Sheet

Name_____Test_____

_____

DIRECTIONS: Fill in the correct answer for each question.

1. (a) (b) (c) (d)   16. (a) (b) (c) (d)
2. (a) (b) (c) (d)   17. (a) (b) (c) (d)
3. (a) (b) (c) (d)   18. (a) (b) (c) (d)
4. (a) (b) (c) (d)   19. (a) (b) (c) (d)
5. (a) (b) (c) (d)   20. (a) (b) (c) (d)

6. (a) (b) (c) (d)   21. (a) (b) (c) (d)
7. (a) (b) (c) (d)   22. (a) (b) (c) (d)
8. (a) (b) (c) (d)   23. (a) (b) (c) (d)
9. (a) (b) (c) (d)   24. (a) (b) (c) (d)
10. (a) (b) (c) (d)   25. (a) (b) (c) (d)

11. (a) (b) (c) (d)
12. (a) (b) (c) (d)
13. (a) (b) (c) (d)
14. (a) (b) (c) (d)
15. (a) (b) (c) (d)

_____

You may wish to go back and check your answers to be sure that you matched the right answer with the right question.

American Red Cross Emergency Water Safety
Answer Key

1. (a) **(b)** (c) (d)
2. (a) (b) **(c)** (d)
3. (a) (b) (c) **(d)**
4. (a) (b) (c) **(d)**
5. **(a)** (b) (c) (d)

6. (a) (b) **(c)** (d)
7. (a) (b) (c) **(d)**
8. (a) (b) (c) **(d)**
9. (a) (b) (c) **(d)**
10. (a) **(b)** (c) (d)

11. (a) **(b)** (c) (d)
12. (a) (b) **(c)** (d)
13. (a) (b) (c) **(d)**
14. (a) (b) **(c)** (d)
15. (a) (b) (c) **(d)**

16. (a) (b) **(c)** (d)
17. (a) (b) (c) **(d)**
18. (a) **(b)** (c) (d)
19. (a) (b) (c) **(d)**
20. **(a)** (b) (c) (d)

21. **(a)** (b) (c) (d)
22. (a) (b) **(c)** (d)
23. (a) **(b)** (c) (d)
24. (a) (b) (c) **(d)**
25. **(a)** (b) (c) (d)

Index